The Empowered Church

Keys to Unlock Explosive Church Growth!

By

H.S. & Mac Mayer

2019

The Empowered Church: Keys to Unlock Explosive Church Growth!

By Mac Mayer

To contact the author for speaking engagements, or for more information, you can access his website at www.macmayer.com

For large quantity orders call 1-877-750-4446

Table of Contents

As a Christian, I care deeply about the Body of Christ and endeavor to see churches flourish and prosper, so more lives are changed worldwide. This book reveals organizational success principles designed to help churches grow. Even though the information is written primarily for the Christian Church, the wisdom can also be applied to nonprofit organizations and businesses so they can experience amazing success as well. I'm praying that this information will be a blessing to those who follow Jesus Christ and want to see lives impacted for God's Kingdom.

Acknowledgment

> *Ask, and it will be given to you; seek, and you will find; knock, and it will be opened to you* (Mt. 7:7 NKJV). *I beseech you therefore, brethren, by the mercies of God, that you present your bodies a living sacrifice, holy, acceptable to God, which is your reasonable service. And do not be conformed to this world, but be transformed by the renewing of our mind, that you may prove what is that good and acceptable and perfect will of God* (Rom. 12:1-2 NKJV).

I started writing this book years ago when a passion rose up within me to see the Church grow and resume its prominent role in society. Throughout this book, I talk about getting wisdom or ideas from God or the Holy Spirit. I know this can seem weird and unsettling to some people. Most of us get a little skittish by people who start every other sentence with, "God told me." I know I do. While I have received counsel that this book would receive more market acceptance if I omitted discussion of who gave me the ideas and content for this book, I want you to know that I must give credit where credit is due—to the Holy Spirit, my Teacher, for giving me the wisdom and knowledge to conceive such powerful concepts. So, I started as the author, gradually reduced to a co-author, and now, hopefully, I can provide a happy little postscript of input. Thank you, Holy Spirit, for letting me write a book with you. And, as you read this book, I hope that you will pray about and receive God's direction on what He would have you do, so that we can connect more hurting people to the transformational power of Jesus and experience more growth in the Body of Christ.

Besides the Holy Spirit, I have a secret weapon I fondly refer to as the Lady Js—three amazingly gifted women God has blessed me with, who assist in my day-to-day business life and especially this writing. Jenny Snyder has been my main assistant for over 16 years. She has the unenviable position of making my total life work, and she does it with diligence and expertise. She has been with me and my wife, Dianne, through many life trials. The second J is our incredible daughter, Jillian Hanes, who is an exceptional technical writer and mother of two of our fantastic grandchildren. The third J that God has most recently blessed me with is Julie Cederlind, who somehow organizes and facilitates my frantic daily schedule at Life Church. She has been a blessing to me with her advanced organizational skills and professionalism.

Words can't express how fortunate and grateful I am for my understanding wife of over 30 years. Somehow Dianne understands and puts up with my compulsion to work, and my attempts to make a difference for the Kingdom. I have also had amazing men in my life including my pastors of over 30 years, who have been excellent role models as men, fathers, and most of all, followers of Jesus. Lynn Schaal in Twin Falls and Mark Boer in Boise, I'm very thankful for your example, patience, and love for me.

Throughout this process, I have prayed for wisdom to convey God's thoughts on the subject of church growth. I am continuing to pray that this writing is a blessing to you and the Body of Christ—His Bride and Church.

Introduction

> *I know God is real and I'm praying for church growth; so, if I'm serving and following God, why isn't this church growing?*
>
> *What do I need to do or change to make our church successful?*
>
> *How can some businesses and civic clubs grow when they* don't *have God, yet many churches are floundering, and we* have *God?*

If you have ever asked these or similar questions, I believe this book can be an answer to your prayers.

This book is written to pastors, church leaders, and individuals who are concerned about where the Christian Church is headed and want to see it regain its position of prominence, influencing lives for the Kingdom of God. I guess I fall into all three categories. I am a pastor, but not a conventional one. I have been a business owner for my entire adult life, starting my first company at 18 years old, and I have been developing and leading businesses for decades. As an individual whose whole life and eternal destiny were changed by Christ, I have been increasingly concerned and perplexed about what is happening to, and causing the decline of, the Christian Church. Maybe you are like me, believing that the Church should be succeeding and prospering. Perhaps you are frustrated that there isn't more growth in your church or that it's not impacting your community. I believe this book can be a resource to help change this.

Many people believe the Church should be flourishing, but they can't quite determine the missing ingredients. Maybe you have been praying and asking what your church can do differently, and you are seeking real solutions. This book is prayerfully designed to help God's people answer those gnawing questions and take the mystery out of church growth and success.

My approach to unraveling this mystery is giving you the principles and practical applications for success. By learning and applying these concepts, your church will grow, and you will be able to transform more lives for the Kingdom of God. When writing, I tend to give you as much information as I can in a concise, easy-to-read, entertaining manner. Of course, I hope that you desire to keep the book as a reference, reading it multiple times and sharing the contents with friends for further discussion. The concepts and success principles within it can be applied to churches, nonprofits and businesses alike. I have developed companies and organizations for 40 years and spent years thinking, praying, and experimenting—sometimes with strong results and other times failing miserably—while developing my ideas on church growth. Now it's a privilege to walk with you, passing along wisdom I have gleaned through my experiences, to help you develop Christ's Church for Kingdom results.

My caveat is this: since I have thought of business and organizational growth since I was a child, I ask you to please give me some grace if I phrase things from a business perspective and don't include 32 Bible references to support my thoughts. My writing style is very personal and straightforward—meaning you won't wonder what I'm saying. That also means I might step on some toes occasionally. I apologize in advance. I feel it is more important to use a more direct approach in conveying my message, rather than being vague simply because I don't want to hurt someone's feelings. The most common responses I have received from this book are: "Thank you. Thank you for taking the mystery out of having a successful church. Thank you for making the information clear, understandable, and practical. School taught me how to deliver a sermon, but it failed to teach me how to build a church."

What this book is not

This book is *not* about theology. Your beliefs are between you and God. Theology is not my department or specialty. If your theology is bad before you read this book, it will be bad after you read this book, and your church will hopefully *not* grow and spread wrong ideas to other people. (Oops, awkward...I may have already stepped on some toes. Don't say I didn't warn you!) Get your beliefs right by seeking the Holy Spirit and studying the Bible. Just because people pass down ideas about God, doesn't mean these ideas are true. This book does *not* replace prayer and the Bible. Prayerfully consider what I'm writing, and implement these concepts based on what you believe God would have you do. I'm trying to do my part in getting information to you; what you do with it is between you and God. This information is proven by time and common sense and is not one-size-fits-all. Nothing replaces prayer and God's wisdom for you in how to implement these ideas.

With this in mind, I pray that this book is a blessing to you, your congregation, and the Body of Christ. I pray that you are abundantly blessed, changing lives for the Kingdom of God, so together we can hear, "Well done, thou good and faithful Church!"

Chapter 1: Picture This

"Is today's church like Kodak?"

There was a long, awkward pause as my mind raced to answer the interviewer's question. I was doing a phone interview, and, up to this point, the questions had been fairly standard. "How did you ever start a real estate appraisal company at eighteen years old when you were basically a high school dropout?" Or, "I understand you had six companies by the time you were twenty-one, would you tell me about that?" Then came the question that made me flinch, "Is today's church like Kodak?"

I can picture the young people reading this slightly tilting their head and, with a furrowed brow, asking, "What's Kodak?" So, let's all brush up on the backstory of Kodak together.

Kodak is a company that makes camera-related products. It started in 1888 and grew to dominate its industry. In 1976 it reportedly had amassed almost 90% of the photographic film sales in the U.S. I know I'm dating myself, but roll film was what they used to develop pictures before you could take unlimited selfies on your iPhones. The film was placed inside a camera, and each picture created an exposure. When the roll was full, it had to be taken into a special store and processed into printed photos. Even with all its previous success, tragically, in 2012

Kodak filed for bankruptcy, and today it is a hollow shadow of its former self. All this happened even though, in 2007, the company had developed an essential element for the future digital camera revolution.[1]

The parallel with Kodak is that at one time most Americans attended a church. The Christian Church had been the mainstay of most American communities. In the post-World War II era, while there were different denominations, the Christian Church—or Body of Christ—was the pillar of our society, with increased religious membership, church funding, and institutional building throughout the 1950s.[2] The Church continues to hold the patented Biblical answers to society's problems for present and future generations. But the Christian Church in the 21st century is generally an anemic, lifeless, black-and-white silhouette of what it once was, and nothing of how it should be influencing lives. So, what do you think? Is there any parallel between Kodak and churches today? Is the Christian Church like Kodak?

I'm not sure how I answered the interviewer's question; however, it has continued to haunt me. Now, upon reflection, I believe yes, *we as the Church have lost our way*. We have not connected and changed with society. That said, the Church is not going to become extinct like a fossilized dinosaur or Kodak camera film. The Church will resurrect—reclaiming its role of impacting lives for the Kingdom. However, we must move past primitive thoughts that people should want film for their wind-up cameras and have real conversations—examining where the Church lost its way and determine how to get it back on track. When we do this, the Church will be more than just a faded photo of a building with a cross. Instead, we will become a vibrant, living collective of active children of God, leading more people to Christ and seeing lives transformed.

A Picture of the Church

Let's take a few minutes to analyze the history and present-day statistics of the American Christian Church. All you academics and history buffs will love this chapter and are silently exclaiming, "Yes!" Before we begin our analysis, I want to assure you that this book is not about dry, boring numbers, and I don't like starting with negative information about how poorly the Church is doing. However, it is crucial to fully understand the problem in Chapter #1, so we can design a solution throughout the rest of the book.

Historically, there are some parallels between Kodak and the Church. There can be no doubt that Judeo-Christian values helped shape the formation of the United States. Christian churches of all varieties played a significant role in America's community life. Christians were at the forefront of major historical events in the United States, including the abolitionist and Civil Rights movements, as well as having a prominent role in the labor movement in America. Christians founded nearly all the first universities in America. In addition, the Third Great Awakening (1858-1859), a period known for religious activism, produced organizations recognized for their continued influence in America today, including the Red Cross, YMCA, and Salvation Army.[2]

How is it that the Church, obviously vital and truly at the head of American culture throughout much of our history, finds itself increasingly irrelevant and at odds with our current society? While the United States is still home to the largest Christian population in the world,[3] and a full 73% of Americans still identify as Christian according to one survey, the number of those who actually practice their faith is approximately 31%.[4]

There may or may not be a quiz at the end of this chapter, so here are a few more stats that describe the Church in America today.

- Millennials (generally defined as those born between the early 1980s-early 2000s) are leaving the Church in droves, and they currently make up the largest segment of unchurched Americans.[5]
- Approximately 59% of millennials who grew up in church will leave.[6]
- The percentage of unchurched people has increased from 44% to 52% in the last decade.[7]
- Nearly half of Americans don't see churches as having a positive impact on their communities.[8]
- Approximately 50% of all churches in America average less than 100 in attendance—40% range from 100-350 attenders, with the remaining 10% having more than 350 in attendance.[9]

While the reason for this apparent ceiling on growth may be in question, the need to address it is not.

The answers proposed in this book directly relate to these noted statistics. If we build our churches with healthy organizational structures, it will reverse the trends of decline and move them to areas of prosperity and influence.

Stay with me through these statistics. Feel free to grab some sugar or caffeine or do some jumping jacks to get your brain on board. It is powerful for us to fully understand the problem so it can catapult us to a solution. The following data is from an article regarding worship attendance, and why many who identify as having a religious affiliation still do not attend church regularly.

Among the growing share of religiously unaffiliated adults in the US, the vast majority say they are not looking for a religion, and relatively few (5%) say they go to services weekly or more often. But what keeps people who have a religious affiliation—that is, who identify with a particular religious group—out of churches?

A 2012 Pew Research poll asked respondents to answer this question in their own words. Among religiously affiliated Americans who say that religion is at least somewhat important in their lives, but who attend worship services no more than a few times a year, 24% cite personal priorities—including 16% who say they are too busy—as reasons they do not attend more often. Another 24% mention practical difficulties, including work conflicts, health problems, or transportation difficulties.

Nearly four in ten (37%) point to an issue directly related to religion or church itself. The most common religion-related responses include disagreements with the beliefs of the religion or their church leaders, or beliefs that attending worship services is not important.[10]

Based on these statistics, just like Kodak, the current Church seems to have lost its way. The public sees the Church as having a product it neither wants nor needs.

Kodak and the Church Lost Their Way

Kodak lost its way when it began to think it was solving the need for film. In reality, it wasn't specifically about the film. While people did need the film, that was just the tangible product they had to purchase to get what they really wanted: to capture those "Kodak moments"—the term which Kodak gave to pictures of special occasions that were worth remembering. Though the company developed the critical element for digital cameras, they failed to effectively capitalize on it, which held them back from becoming one of the main competitors of capturing images in the new technological era. If companies and organizations want to stay relevant, they need to understand the changing needs of society and be able to meet them.

Likewise, some pastors may feel they are fulfilling the need for conducting a church service. At one time this was a real necessity because the primary way for people to receive information about God was for them to physically come together and meet for a church service. However, in the current digital age, people don't need to gather as they used to in order to gain information. There are thousands upon thousands of the latest and greatest preaching and teaching on Podcasts and YouTube videos available 24/7 with the touch of a button. Now I'm speaking your language, aren't I? Also, just gathering together and listening to someone talk doesn't necessarily solve peoples' real needs or connect them with God. Unfortunately, they might not think of God as a need anyway, as the number of religiously unaffiliated Americans continues to grow. The percentage of adults (ages 18 and older) who describe themselves as Christians dropped from 78.4% in 2007 to 70.6% in 2014. Over the same period, the percentage of Americans who are religiously unaffiliated—describing themselves as atheist, agnostic or "nothing in particular"—has jumped more than six points, from 16.1% to 22.8%. [11]

These numbers are dramatic because they represent *millions* of people walking away from the Church in a relatively short period. These trends are a genuine reflection of how people perceive the Church, as having little value to offer them. The numbers are significant but not irreversible.

Chapter 1 Reflection Questions

1. What do you think about the condition of the local church?

2. How have you seen the Church lose its way?

3. What need is the Church actually fulfilling?

[1] https://petapixel.com/2018/06/14/a-brief-history-of-kodak-the-camera-giants-rise-and-fall/ accessed 11/19/2018

[2] https://probe.org/the-social-and-historical-impact-of-christianity/ accessed 09/18/2018

[3] https://en.wikipedia.org/wiki/Christianity_by_country accessed 09/18/2018

[4] https://www.barna.com/research/state-church-2016/ accessed 09/17/2018

[5] https://www.barna.com/research/the-priorities-challenges-and-trends-in-youth-ministry/ accessed 02/01/2019

[6] https://www.barna.com/research/5-reasons-millennials-stay-connected-to-church/ accessed 02/01/2019

[7] https://www.barna.com/research/the-priorities-challenges-and-trends-in-youth-ministry/ accessed 09/18/2018

[8] https://reachrightstudios.com/9-important-church-statistics-2017/ accessed 09/18/2018

[9] https://thomrainer.com/2015/03/one-key-reason-churches-exceed-350-average-attendance/ accessed 09/18/2018

[10] http://www.pewresearch.org/fact-tank/2013/09/13/what-surveys-say-about-worship-attendance-and-why-some-stay-home/ accessed 09/18/2018

[11] (http://www.pewforum.org/2015/05/12/americas-changing-religious-landscape/ accessed 04/20/2018)

Chapter 2: What Are We Here For?

Right or wrong, perceptions are people's reality. Think about how society views the Church of today and its product. Some people might think that church attendees are a bunch of out-of-touch, critical, condemning hypocrites. They dress in uncomfortable clothes, sit on uncomfortable chairs, and listen to boring condemning talks. If you go to a church, they ask for your money and the next thing you know, you're cleaning the church and mowing the lawn on your days off. Nobody has fun, and smiling is certainly not allowed. Attendees are grumpy old people that drive beat-up cars with a faded "Jesus Loves You" bumper sticker next to an old fossil outline where a fish emblem used to be. I know this is not true about most churches, but that doesn't matter. What matters is people's perception.

Since 2010, millennials' views of churches and religious organizations as having a positive effect on society has dropped 18%—from a favorability rating of 73% down to 55% today.[1] Perception to them is the reality that is keeping them away. Obviously, much of the perception has been misrepresented by media and sources determined to undermine the truth of the Gospel through negative news programs or isolated situations. Beliefs about the Church are shaped more by negative news or mistakes individuals have made, rather than how people have been set free from addictions, marriages salvaged, and lives saved because of the love of Jesus. Instead, how many times have you heard something similar to this? *News flash: Pastor embezzled millions of dollars to support his extravagant lifestyle, investigator finds he has more wives than Solomon.* The news goes on to say that people with beat-up cars and fossilized fish emblems supported his extravagant lifestyle. Was the newscast correct? Perhaps yes, perhaps no, but that's not the point. What is the Church doing to actively change these false viewpoints and perceptions?

Negative is Good!

Here is the great news: if we are a little different than the phony Christians fabricated on TV sitcoms or the news, it will be a refreshing change for most people. Think of this negative public perception toward churches and Christians as an advantage. No church can have all the negative attributes that are portrayed in the media and on TV, so we are already way ahead! But what if the Church was a positive environment and the opposite of what is portrayed? What if new attendees came into churches and felt loved and cared for? What if they thought we were more interested in serving them and helping them solve their problems, instead of our own? People would walk back outside, check the sign above the door thinking, "Well it says church, but this is nothing like the negative reports I've heard. These people are nice! They didn't ask me for the PIN for my debit card. They have answers to my life problems. Wow, I like this place! I should tell my friends."

Great News #2: Society is Really Messed Up!

Building a successful church shouldn't be difficult if we take our eyes off ourselves and instead look at other people's needs. Society is amazingly messed up; people have masses of problems. That's great news! They have piles of difficulties, and there is only one place where they can get *real* answers. Jesus. Think of all the issues people are facing today: sexual immorality is rampant, opioid abuse is at crisis levels, there are financial issues, high divorce rates, health problems, bullying, identity confusion, and the list goes on and on. All these things can be answered by a healthy, functioning church, pointing people to a relationship with Jesus and the solutions He provides.

Typical Couple

Imagine an average unchurched couple thinking about their life. They wake up one beautiful, warm Sunday morning and the wife says to her husband, "Gee, Dear. I love our life! Everything is perfect. Our marriage is great, our finances are great, our kids are great—having no personal or academic issues. The whole world seems to be peaceful and getting along. Life is just grand! What do you say we get out of this comfy, warm bed and drive across town to that strange building with the cross on it, where all those people meet each week? You know, the place where we don't know anyone, and they don't talk, dress, or act like us, and rumor has it they don't even like us?"

The husband replies, "Gee, Honey. That's a great idea! I don't have anything else to do on my only day off from work. Let me jump up and get dressed. I'm sure the kids won't mind when I drag them out of *their* warm comfy beds, after a late Saturday night of fun and movies. Then we'll all drive down there happily together."

Not Likely.

Their thoughts or words may go more like this: "Hon, I'm nervous. It doesn't seem like life is working out. This is not how I thought things would be. Our lives are unsettled, we aren't communicating well in our marriage, the kids are out of control. I don't trust the schools or politicians. I feel stressed out. I'm worried about our finances, my job, terrorism, and the economy. I don't know what to do. I wonder if there is anything to the whole God thing. We've tried almost everything except God. I think He is my last hope. What do you think about going to one of those churches? Maybe they can help."

So this brave couple struggles past their fears to drive up to a strange place, with unfamiliar people, and what is their experience? Will it be a stagnant, lifeless reunion of the Walking Dead or a place of joyful answers? Will it be a dated photographic answer from another era or a vibrant, ageless solution that will relate to them today and change their eternity forever? Will they be accepted and loved? Will they get help and their needs met, or will they swear on their TV remote to never try that again? We need to have real solutions for a world that is lost and hurting, and we need to present it in a relevant way so they can receive it. They don't know they are lost, but they do know things aren't working out, because without God, how can they?

Yeah...Dying is Not on My List Today!

We proclaim Jesus as the answer to life. However, what does the public see Jesus as an answer to? If society has heard anything about Jesus, it may be that He is the answer to the life *after* this one. They may believe the only solution Jesus provides applies to dying. While it's true that accepting Jesus is a choice that affects us for eternity, it might not be relatable to people overwhelmed with life *today.* People have the mindset, "I'm just trying to survive this day and this week." Their daily to-do list looks something like this: work, grab treats for the school party, pick up the kids after school, rush them to the dentist, race home to prepare dinner, drop them off at soccer practice, pick them up from practice, eat dinner, help kids with their homework, fold a load of laundry, wash the dishes, and then catch an episode of reality TV before passing out in bed.

With a list like this, dying isn't even on their radar. They don't have time to think about something so permanent. Sure, they might briefly consider their mortality with the passing of a close friend or loved one, but the Attention Deficit Disorder of life quickly pulls them back, making them feel they can put off an eternal decision until later. Some resolve, "Maybe before major surgery or when I'm one hundred and three years old, I'll check back with the whole Jesus and God thing, but since it's not on my list of things to do, I'm good. I better get started on the things that affect my life now."

The Problem is the Answer

If we as the Church are looking for societal needs to meet, we really shouldn't have to look very far. There are millions of people homeless and on drugs; seniors suffering on limited incomes; and grieving people struggling with family deaths, divorce, and post-abortion loss. Still others are trapped in pornography, illicit relationships, and substance abuse. The world's cup of turmoil and problems is running over, and we sit idle, complaining that our church isn't growing. Can you say, *Awkward?!?*

Opposites Attract

As we have talked about, the world has a stereotyped perception of who the Church is and what we do. If we want to attract the world to us, all we must do is be the opposite of what the media says we are. The great news is that is just what Jesus has called us to be. The world believes we are condemning, hateful hypocrites, standing against a host of things they deem perfectly acceptable. What if we were defined not by what we were against, but by how much we loved people? What if we acted like Christ's followers, *actually* following His example? Jesus demonstrated love and acceptance of people, precisely as they were, as He told them, "Neither do I condemn you; go and sin no more." (John 8:11b NKJV) If we love people that much, we will want to love them through their junk.

The world believes we sit in dreary, guilt-inducing churches. What if our services were encouraging and provided life answers? God is our Father, so there is nothing about our universe that is boring! Let's have exciting, appealing services; having fun is not a sin. The world thinks churches don't actually *do* anything. What if we got activated and went out into our community and made a loving difference? Many of the arguments against the Church and its irrelevance are correct, so let's change. Opposites will attract. Those in the darkness will seek the light. If we want to be that "light of the world" that Christ called us to be, we should listen to people's complaints about us and be willing to change our presentation without changing the content and our core beliefs (Matthew 5:14 NKJV).

Where is Your Focus?

I have asked some people in church leadership: are you self/church-focused or others-focused? I might get this pious response: "Brother Mac, we are others-focused. We are focused on those poor spiritual wretches headed toward the fiery gates of Hell where they will forever be separated from an all-loving God for eternity." Okay,

I love the answer. Since you are others-focused, how is that going for you? Who are the people you are serving and what needs are you meeting? If we are fishers of men, how plentiful is your catch or impact on people? I can tell the results of a fishing trip by the haul. Are your nets bulging over capacity and are you calling for other churches to help you bring in all the changed lives? Oops, is that a deafening silence I hear? If we cannot see tangible results from our ministry, we are doing something wrong.

Negotiable and Non-Negotiable

We need to analyze what is negotiable about who we are as a church and the elements of our services, and what is non-negotiable. What flexibility do we have? Based on Jesus' ministry style, I would say we have a lot of flexibility on how we approach ministry, definitely more than what we are using. Jesus didn't even do most of his ministry in a building. He did it on a seashore, in houses, or under a tree. I'm not sure what hymnal Jesus used to lead praise and worship for his posse...Oh that's right, He didn't. Well, it sounds like Jesus watered down His message then. Hardly. My point is, can we please open our minds a smidge to some things that could be negotiable so that we can present the non-negotiable goodness of God to more people?

Crossroads Church, based in Cincinnati, has been named the fastest growing church in America twice in the last five years. The church functions like a startup and has been described as "an entrepreneurial church and a church for entrepreneurs." For those not in the business industry, a startup is a new company, typically designed to solve a specific problem or fill a void in the marketplace. Think Facebook, Uber, eBay or even Amazon. Concerning the way their church functions, senior pastor Brian Tome says, "We don't set out to intentionally disrupt anything...But Jesus said he works in new wineskins. He's not against old wineskins. But he said he has come to do a new thing. The Holy Spirit is active in our church, causing us to do things other churches aren't willing to do."[2]

What Are We Here For?

As previously stated, the Church is generally judged by what we are against instead of what we are for. Perhaps we deserve that for failing to heed one of our primary assignments. We are commanded to love people as Jesus does. "Let me give you a new command: Love one another. In the same way I loved you, you love one another. This is how everyone will recognize that you are my disciples—when they see the love you have for each other." John 13:34-35 (MSG) This does not mean embracing or rationalizing sin. It does mean actively loving people where they are and helping them get free of their bondage and connect with God. Often, it seems the Church gets so caught up in our agenda of having a church service (like Kodak was in manufacturing film), that we don't see a world literally crying out for answers that we can provide.

When considering the details of our fictitious typical couple's lives earlier on in this chapter, we can see that people have all sorts of critical needs that the Church can and should be helping to solve. I don't want to get political on you, but one reason the welfare system is in such a ginormous state of waste is that the Church did not do its appointed job of taking care of the widows, orphans, and people in need. We relinquished our responsibility, and the government came in to cover for us in their typical, less-than-efficient bureaucratic way of doing things. This also happened with the education system and many other social structures. There is a multitude of societal needs that should be provided for by the Church. The great news is that Father God has equipped us with the Holy Spirit, who has the wisdom to solve all these problems if we ask.

Many churches are accomplishing great things by meeting needs. Not only are they helping people, but they are growing and flourishing as well. When I talk about the Church, I'm generalizing to make the point that just like Kodak, it is easy to lose our way. Statistics show that most churches have lost their way and their attendance is declining. "The drop in the Christian share of the population has been driven mainly by declines among mainline Protestants and Catholics. Each of those large religious traditions has shrunk by approximately three percentage points since 2007." [3] Many churches are doing a great job but, unfortunately, they are a small minority. These thriving churches have discovered what God would have them do, and they are actively doing their part in tangibly meeting needs and changing lives. They are feeding the homeless, getting people off drugs, helping with housing and job needs. They are ministering to people in hospitals, nursing homes, jails, and prisons. They are counseling people going through divorce and life's tragic situations. Because these churches are serving people's needs first, it is opening the door for them to introduce them to Jesus. For the rest of us, we need to find out what needs we can and should be meeting and get a move on!

Chapter 2 Reflection Questions

1. What is the atmosphere of your church—encouraging and welcoming, or boring and condemning? Be honest—even if it's painful!

2. What needs do you see in your local community?

3. When it comes to meeting those needs, what is the Church doing that is working? How can they do more of it?

[1]http://www.pewresearch.org/fact-tank/2016/01/04/millennials-views-of-news-media-religious-organizations-grow-more-negative accessed 09/20/2018

[2]https://www.christianitytoday.com/ct/2018/may/crossroads-cincinnati-america-fastest-growing-church-start.html accessed 09/20/2018

[3] http://www.pewforum.org/2015/05/12/americas-changing-religious-landscape/ accessed 04/19/2018

Chapter 3: The Family Business

While we now have the connections, education, and societal permission to pursue a career path of our choice, up until just a few decades ago it was a tradition and expected for children to join the family business. Parents would teach their children "tricks of the trade" correlating to their specific industry. They would pass down family recipes in the restaurant business, teach certain farming techniques, or, in my family's case, our kids grew up and worked in the business we were developing.

Jesus was part of two family businesses—carpentry for His earthly father, Joseph, as well as doing the Lord's business (Mark 6:3, Luke 2:49). After being lost for three days when he was 12 years old, Jesus' parents found Him in the temple, conversing with the teachers. When His parents began to question Him, Jesus replied, "Did you not know that I must be about My Father's business?" (Luke 2:41-49 NKJV) This had to seem a little awkward to Joseph because Jesus was not selling furniture for Joseph & Sons Furniture Manufacturing LLC. How is a parent supposed to respond to that? I don't think they cover that in Parenting 101.

So what is the Father's business? The Father's business is doing what we see the Father doing. Jesus explains this in John 5:19, "I tell you the truth, the Son can do nothing by Himself. He does only what He sees the Father doing. Whatever the Father does, the Son also does." (NLT) If God is our Father, and God is love, then

His business is all about loving people and changing lives (John 1:12, 1 John 4:16b). Jesus was all about His Father's business. As the Son of God, Jesus did His part, and now He said it is up to us to continue the family heritage of loving others and changing lives. This is the family business. It should be our business or profession to develop the Church—not the building, but the body of believers. The Church is not a building; any structure or place will work for regular gatherings. The Church is the body of believers.

So my "business" is to love and develop the people (who may attend at a location or building we commonly call a church) into a thriving, outreaching group that follows Jesus. Once empowered, this Body of Christ—the real Church—will go about loving, helping, and healing individuals, families, and entire communities.

Membership Problems

I was having dinner with Pastor Paul, the senior pastor of a large church in Hong Kong. I said, "Pastor Paul, what problems are you having at your church?" He replied, "Mac, we put on huge outreach events that draw many people. People come from everywhere, but after the event, the people don't join our church." I listened to Pastor Paul and then asked what seemed like a really dumb question. "Why do you want the people to join your church?" I saw him sputter and twitch like I was holding my chopsticks upside down. I'm sure he was thinking, "Duh, this goofy American consultant can't figure out why I want people to join our church. They are really slow in that country." Before he could answer, I said, "In America, I might be able to get people to join my church, but after they do, they may never come back again. So what is the big deal about having them join the church if they quit and never return?" He nodded his head slowly at the truth of this reality: that people could be members on paper, but never return.

All our efforts to get more people in the door is a waste of time if we don't have the right motives as an others-focused church, and the coinciding actions of providing the follow-up care they need. I continued, "What if instead of wasting time on trying to get them to join your church, we spend our time connecting with them, finding out who they are, and how we can help them have a more meaningful life? What if we spend time relating to them and guiding them to a better future? What will have more impact on them staying in your church, if you talk them into signing a membership form, or you capture their heart because they know you care about them and can tangibly help them?" Pastor Paul said, "Yes, Mac. If we have a heart connection, they will stay." Right on, Pastor Paul!

Problem-Solving

The concept that I was trying to get across to Pastor Paul is a basic business tenet that absolutely applies to the success of the local church. Since we are about our Father's business and we want to be successful, let's discuss some general business principles. The basic tenet for a company to function and be successful is to find a need and fill it. Business is all about problem solving. Every company exists to solve someone's real or perceived needs or problems. If I have peeling paint on my house, I have many options with which to remedy it. There are a variety of businesses to help me solve this issue. I can buy the supplies and do it myself, or I can call a host of contractors to solve the problem for me at a variety of different price points. Another option is that I can re-side my house, so I never have to repaint it. I could also sell this house and move somewhere else, or even tear the whole thing down and build a new one. The options I can choose and the amount of money I can spend to solve the problem of peeling paint are nearly limitless.

People have needs far beyond what the business world can solve though. As we have discussed, life can be very challenging, and there is a litany of problems and needs to address. Nearly everyone deals with worry, stress, loneliness, pain, and a host of other negative emotions at some point. People are looking for answers to these and many other troubles, and the array of solutions to choose from is vast. Some of those answers could include stopping by the local bar, starting an illicit relationship, getting a prescription, or perhaps even visiting a local church. A word of caution—some of these potential answers may cause more problems than they solve, much like all the new drug prescriptions they are advertising on TV. "This product will cure your dry skin! However, potentially harmful side effects include..." BIG breath before rattling off the following list as fast as a professional auctioneer, "...diarrhea, blurred vision, your right arm could fall off, your teeth fall out, and you could die. You should not drive a car or operate heavy equipment until you know how this drug affects you. Ask your doctor about a new prescription today!" Aren't you glad there are no adverse side effects to the Gospel of Jesus Christ?

Just like in the business world, our success in running and succeeding with the Father's business is about us focusing on and solving other people's needs. In the business world, the more people that we can help solve their problems, the more successful our company will be. Similarly, the better the Church is at meeting others' needs, the more successful we will ultimately be.

Focus

"Membership" isn't a dirty word. I'm not against churches growing their membership; that's not the point. I don't care what churches decide on this issue. I am against us continuing to look at just what *we* want while ignoring people who are crying out for help. Our energy will go toward whatever we focus on. If I'm focused on what I want—increased membership at my church—I can't simultaneously give my full attention to what others need and want, which is getting their life problems solved. If I love and care for people effectively at my church, I won't be able to get them to leave. Pretty soon they will be bringing all their friends over to be part of my church. It's like ministering to cats. I can put a collar around a cat's neck and stamp "Member" on its tag indicating he belongs to me, and he will typically wander away. Or I can put a bowl of milk on my patio. The only problem with the bowl of milk on my patio is that soon I will need multiple containers, a larger patio, and an exponential increase in my milk budget since the first cat will bring every cat in the neighborhood to my backyard. I'm not saying people are like cats, but then again...maybe I am.

The Law of Exchange

Taking the idea of solving people's problems a step further, let's revert to business terminology. The law of exchange is at the core of a successful business. A customer says, "I want your product or service to solve my need more than I want the time and money it would cost me to solve the problem myself." When I teach companies or organizations how to succeed, one fundamental element of human behavior and the free enterprise system they need to understand is the law of exchange. The law of exchange is applied subconsciously, and we do it continuously for almost everything in life. When a person decides to shop at a business, they are subconsciously putting this law into play. Their mind is automatically calculating a multitude of different equations to determine where they are going to shop, and how much it is ultimately going to cost them. Cost is more than money and does not equate solely to dollars and cents. The total cost is a combination of everything I'm giving up, including time, effort, other opportunities, possibly even my dignity to get the result I'm seeking.

Here's how it works. Say I want popcorn. There are a whole host of ways I can get popcorn, and all of them have substantially different total costs and results. First, I can go to a store and get popcorn to pop; even within this option, I have several alternatives. I can drive across town and get the cheapest popcorn per kernel from the big box discount or club warehouse. The advantage is that I can get a 35-gallon drum of unpopped kernels for approximately $10. I'm not sure what I'll do with 35 pounds of unpopped kernels, but by the time it's popped it would be enough to serve the fans at an average Pittsburgh Steelers football game. Basically, I would have a lifetime supply of popcorn. However, there is more to the cost than the $10 I pay. Getting the popcorn I would have to devote a half day of my life to obtain it, and I have no idea where I'd store the popcorn once I got it home.

My next option is that I can go to the local convenience store. They sell a baggy of 28 kernels for $2.95. This is considerably less product, my overall cost is also less, no storage problems, and it would take way less time to buy with no marathon hike involved.

Another alternative is to fill my car up with gas at the same convenience store, and with a full tank of gas, I get a free bag of popcorn already cooked. It's in a container about the size of a test tube, but it's "free" with the fill-up. So if I spend $75 on gas, the same 28 kernels are already popped, and it didn't cost me anything...sort of.

A fantastic option is that I can take my awesome wife on a date to the movie theater. If we go in the afternoon, the matinee should only cost us about $50 for the two of us, and then we get a large refillable popcorn bucket for another $25. The people are friendly, the popcorn is fresh, I get to spend time with my wife, and the deciding bonus is I get out of mowing the lawn. This is the best value for my time.

Why do I tell you all this stuff? Is it because you should start giving away popcorn at church? Probably not. I want you to understand that there is intense competition for people's time. When you are asking a person to attend church, you are asking them not to be at their best friend's house eating chips, drinking a beverage, and watching the big game on TV. They can't sleep in and have a leisurely brunch with their spouse while perusing the latest real estate magazine. They can't attend church with you while at the same time catching up on housework and paying some bills.

Everything competes with everything else; there are costs and benefits to everything. I know it shouldn't be that way regarding the awesomeness of God and church, but it is. Life is so busy, and there is an endless number of things we can do with our time. We could exercise, play video games, take a nap, work, hang out on social media, go for a drive, talk on the phone, go to the park, go to church, etc. but we have to choose because we can't do them all at the same time.

The good news is that as the Church, we have a massively unfair advantage representing God. There shouldn't be any competition regarding where people choose to spend their time. When I say this, some of you are completely missing what I'm saying. You may be thinking that I'm talking about creating an event or performance, but that's not at all what I'm saying. The truth is, many of us have been terrible representatives of the Father's business. We have taken the most significant event in history that has the potential to alter the eternal destiny of every man, woman, boy, and girl on earth, and presented it as a boring church service. Father, please forgive us. Many of us should be sued for misrepresentation and closed down. This does not mean I'm about creating a Hollywood performance; that's not the real answer. Read on. We need to give people so much value for their time that there is nowhere else they want to be.

Let's listen in on a possible phone conversation between best friends: "No, Ted. I'm not coming over to your house until after church to watch the big game. I know I'll miss watching my favorite team play the first half of the championships—the best game of the year—but Ted, you don't understand. Since Cindy and I have been attending church, our marriage is better, we have met these amazing people that love, accept, and encourage us, and we have learned how to pay off our bills and are prospering more than ever. Plus, our kids love it there. They would never let us miss. Most of all, Ted, we now have an amazing relationship with God, the Creator of the Universe. Having so much peace and fulfillment is incredible. Ted, the Church has even helped us discover our gifts and abilities, and God is using us to touch lives in a meaningful and powerful way. Cindy finally feels fulfilled since she is ministering to unwed, pregnant teenage girls, and I have guys on the usher's team who are role models for me. There is no way we are missing church. The price is far too high. What's that, Ted? You and Mary are looking for a change in your lives too? Sure you can come to church with us! That would be great, and then we can watch the second half of the game together."

Even though it appears we have worldly competition for the Father's business, in fact, it's no contest. Jesus is the only true answer. That is why it is crazy that we don't have people waiting in line to attend our services. What it shows is that we don't know what we have or how to represent it to a hurting public. If we are others-focused and develop Biblical answers to their problems, there will be no end to the market success we will have in influencing people for the Kingdom.

Cost vs. Value

Before we can be influential in people's lives, we must address the issue of the intangible costs people pay coming to our church, and how to bring value to their experience so they want to stay. As previously mentioned, cost is not only money and time, but it can also include being inconvenienced or uncomfortable, possibly being embarrassed, etc. If a business or a church is hard to get to, has inadequate parking, rude people, is boring, or difficult to navigate, these are all part of the cost someone "pays" to get our product or service. If we make it challenging for people to attend, we are creating friction points. Every business or church has friction points. The better we are at removing these obstacles and the more value we provide for their lives, the more they will seek us out.

Look at Amazon and their incredible business success. People can order almost any product from any company, any time of day from their phone. The order is placed with one click and delivered to their door at a competitive price. Is there any question why Amazon is such a huge success? When we give people a product of great value while lowering the resistance or friction for them to receive it, they will be beating a path to our door and bringing their friends. Of course, eliminating friction points while offering a watered-down message of the Gospel would be counterproductive, diminishing the value that Jesus brings to people's lives.

The Law of Exchange—A Different Perspective

Real, life-changing results are the valued commodity that people will continue exchanging their free time for, thus the law of exchange unquestionably applies to churches. It's Sunday morning or Saturday-Sabbath, shoot it could be Tuesday at midnight. I don't care when you worship. Anyway, it's Frank and Sally's only day off work. It's a beautiful spring day, maybe the first warm day after a cold hard winter, and they are considering what they should do for the day. They are subconsciously calculating in their minds if they should go to church or do something else. Thousands of thoughts are streaming through their brains. Frank muses, "Wow, these sheets feel great. I never get to sleep in. This is my only day off all week. I need a break. It's been a tough week, and I want to reward myself with golf." Sally thinks, "I have piles of laundry, the house needs to be cleaned, and we have no food in the fridge." Notice how Frank considers playing, and Sally must do all the work. Oops, I digress. In any case, Frank and Sally think about what they would be exchanging their time for in order to attend church. Sally says, "Frank let's get up. Going to church always makes me feel great. There is no place we would rather be on our day off than getting real answers to improve our lives in a great, accepting environment with our closest friends. Plus, God uses us to impact the lives of others there too." That's one set of thoughts they could be thinking. Or they could think of church, pull the pillow over their head, and moan before going back to sleep.

Duty or Value

Some people will attend church out of obligation or because they are guilted into attending. "By golly, my parents suffered and went to this church all their life, so we can endure it and make our kids suffer through it too." Guilt is a terrible motivator; I don't want people showing up because I shamed them into coming. On a side note, statistics prove that Baby Boomers are far more likely to attend church out of guilt, habit, or some other reason, rather than millennials, who have no qualms with avoiding church altogether if they find no value in it.[1] The first chance they get to bolt out the door, they will. I would too if guilt was my primary motivation. People should not be coerced to attend church out of duty, shame, condemnation, or guilt, because if they are, they won't stay.

Our Solution is Solving Their Need

The Church has the best product: Jesus! Yes, He truly is the solution to society's most significant problems as "the way, the truth, and the life," filling the void that religions and self-help books can never fill (John 14:6 NKJV). If we combine the value Jesus offers with our main desires to A) have a healthy, growing church and B) fulfill the call of God on our lives by "making disciples of all nations," we conclude that the problems in society are catalysts to achieving what we want (Matthew 28:19).

We should start with what people want and need (answers to life problems), and not force our agenda (church growth) on them. When we help meet their basic needs, it builds our relationship and credibility with them so they will be much more open to receiving our help in other areas of their life, i.e., introducing them to Jesus. I was always taught: “If you help enough people get what they want, you will get what you want.” So if we take our eyes off what we want and help society with their needs—being about our Father’s business—we can end up with a thriving church full of devoted followers of Christ.

Chapter 3 Reflection Questions

1. There are costs and benefits to everything. How does the law of exchange relate to your spiritual life?

2. What would make your church more valuable to your community?

3. What friction points do you need to remove for people? Analyze your church from the street, parking lot, main entrance, and all the way through the service. What does a guest experience?

[1]https://www.barna.com/research/americans-divided-on-the-importance-of-church/#.UzOeP_ldVqG accessed 09/20/2018

Chapter 4: Flip This Church

I Couldn't Be the Problem

One conversation, and the resulting question, I have heard several times lately goes like this: "Mac, we have an awesome pastor. He loves God, loves us, and presents the Bible to the best of his knowledge and abilities. We have been praying and believing God would grow our church for years, but there is no actual growth happening. Nobody wants to talk about this ultra-obvious issue of why we aren't growing. People are losing hope. Mac, why do you think we aren't growing?" First, I'm honored they think I would have a reflection on this. Without looking deeper and seeking insight from the Holy Spirit, I would be arrogant to presume I know the answer. However, as a problem-solver, I do love that they are asking such a great question. This is very healthy. If we aren't asking questions, we probably won't be getting answers.

However, within their comments, I hear the underlying assumption that the problem couldn't be with them. They are doing their part right, and they are just waiting for God to wake up from His extended nap and bless the place. It's all about God, and when He wants the place to grow, it will. They are waiting and praying for God to send the people to their church; growth is all up to God and His timing.

This sounds very spiritual. The only problem is, it removes the emphasis of "us" having to change or do anything different. After all, it couldn't be that we are the reason the church isn't growing. It must be God or society or something—anything except us. Perhaps they're thinking, "I know the reason this church isn't growing can't be us. We have been doing church this way since the early nineteen hundreds, and the church was growing then. We have been faithful and haven't changed a thing—the place is decorated and looks the same, we use the same hymnals and sing the same songs. In fact, we still have the same greeters and pipe organ. It must be God! We have done our part to remain faithful and not change a thing."

The Answer

Their blessed assurance that "they are doing everything right and when God does His part the place will finally grow" may not be the most helpful viewpoint. The Father says in His Word that He loves the whole world and He wants all to come to know Jesus as Savior (John 3:16, 1 Timothy 2:3b-4). God's heart is full of love for us and not only does He want everyone to accept Jesus and spend eternity with Him, but He wants us to do well on earth too. The Father wants us to be in a great church where we will be loved and taken care of, so it seems all the changes must be on our end (Hebrews 10:25).

This leads us to the matter of stewardship. I feel that if I'm not doing every possible thing to be a good steward of the people God brings to me, then He shouldn't bring me any more. Instead, He should send them to some other church where they will be properly fed and nurtured. Imagine the Father is waiting on us and saying, "I would love to bless that church with people and growth, but every time I send people to them, the people end up leaving because they don't relate to them, and they don't take care of them by loving them and meeting their needs. If they would make changes and be a better steward of the people I send them, I would send them more."

Flip This Church

Reality shows are an extremely popular television genre. Some of them are based on the concept of transformations. The theme of the show goes like this: there is a business, usually a restaurant, that is failing miserably—employee turnover has skyrocketed, the food is terrible, finances are a wreck, and 50's style urban dejection is the décor of choice. The employees that do bother to show up to work are drinking on the job, rude to customers, or do the bare minimum to get a paycheck while maintaining their lousy attitude. The owners don't know how to make things better, and the third-generation business is on the verge of closing.

Some elements of this remind me of the Kodak concept and the local church. In one of these shows, a restaurant specialist and his team swoop in and make the necessary changes for success. The team has free rein to do what they want. They tear out walls and redecorate the place; they fire some staff and coach others; they revamp the menu and get the finances in order. Soon they reopen the doors and people are standing in line to be part of this new business that has determined to serve their local community better. As the show comes to an end, we have the feeling that the restaurant has successfully made its turnaround and will continue to flourish. Experience tells us that some of these businesses will slip back into their previous bad habits and eventually close. Others will keep their new solutions and successfully serve their community for decades to come.

Would the turnaround idea work with churches? What if some of the great church builders of our age, like Andy

Stanley (North Point Community Church), Rick Warren (Saddleback Church), Chris Hodges (Church of the Highlands), or Steven Furtick (Elevation Church) could come into struggling churches with their leadership team and make significant changes? What would the result be? We can only speculate, but based on their track record, they have the necessary wisdom and knowledge to make the churches successful, and, since they have done it once they can do it again. We also know they have coached and influenced thousands of other churches to make changes so they could thrive. So what does this have to do with growing our own church?

The Leadership Principle

Pastor and best-selling author, John Maxwell, is an amazing man who has devoted his life to helping others succeed. He has written over 70 books [1] and has positively impacted millions of lives. In 2014, he was named the number-one leadership and management expert in the world by Inc Magazine.[2] I believe one of Maxwell's most powerful and poignant quotes from his book, *The 21 Irrefutable Laws of Leadership* is, "Everything rises and falls on leadership." This saying applies to the restaurant turnaround in our previous example, and everything else we do, individually and corporately, including church turnarounds, growth, and success.

If we blame God for our lack of growth, we are abdicating our responsibility to lead well. It wouldn't make sense if the owner of the failing restaurant said, "Hey, I won't change my business! I will just pray and believe God will bring the people into my unfriendly, ugly atmosphere to eat my unpalatable food." We would think the person was crazy, and yet we go back to our church and say the same thing. We might be serving our attendees unpalatable spiritual food in a less than welcoming and not so healthy environment and wonder why they don't stay. Businesses, civic clubs, and organizations of all kinds rise or fall based, to a significant extent, on their leadership. Why would churches be any different?

I'm not a betting man, but if I were, I would wager that if the right leader came into most churches and had the freedom to make enough changes, it would grow. Let me pose the reverse scenario from a business standpoint: name all the businesses you know throughout the history of the world that continued to grow and prosper year after year and had terrible, inept leadership? Is that a deafening silence I hear? You're right; there hasn't been one! It is an impossible outcome. You can't do incompetent things and have long-term success. There might be some short-term wins, but everything soon balances out, and the leadership principle is proven to be true. This principle also applies to churches.

Now, I'm not saying that if your church isn't growing, you need to replace your pastor. Most pastors would love to see their church grow; however, their board, denomination, or congregation may not be comfortable with the changes necessary for growth to happen. When I say leadership, there is a tendency to think of the head of the organization automatically. While there is some truth to that, the reality is that "leadership" encompasses the whole group of influencers in a church or organization. Don't think that changing pastors is the answer. Instead, consider that having the right leadership team and mentality could be the solution. Just as a side note, churches will never be successful if they keep changing leaders. The larger an entity, the longer it takes to make changes, and if you keep changing the leader at the helm of the church every couple of years, you will be wandering all over in an ocean of confusion. It takes time for a leader to verbalize a vision and assemble a team around him or her for church success to happen. Support your leader to build a great team and make the necessary changes for ongoing Kingdom success.

All About Management

One key concept in the investment industry is: "Before investing in a company, you always look at the management." If the management is strong, the chances are excellent that the company growth will be strong. The key takeaway is that great leaders know how to develop winning teams that, in turn, build winning organizations. We will cover this in more detail throughout the rest of the book.

Change Them, Not Me

One significant problem leadership faces that I have alluded to, is that no one really *wants* to change. This is especially true in the institutional church. We might say the words out one side of our mouth, "Yes, we want to grow!" and out the other side, we say, "As long as it's not uncomfortable and we don't have to actually do anything different, and certainly as long as no one sits in *my* seat on a Sunday morning." The attitude of "Yes, I believe in change, as long as it's with others and it doesn't affect me in any way," reflects where a lot of us are regarding church growth.

Yes, this might be uncomfortable to read, but consider it tough love. Isn't it strange that we have been instructed to win the lost, and then we place a PS? "Sure as long as we don't have to change anything, including accepting those wayward unbelievers into our church because they might mess things up. If those sinners will clean up their lives and become Pharisees like us, we will let them come into our church." It's like saying, you must take a bath and clean up thoroughly, before you're allowed to take a shower.

The reality is that unbelievers are messy. Proverbs 14:4 says, "The only clean stable is an empty stable. So if you want the work of an ox and to enjoy an abundant harvest, you'll have a mess or two to clean up!" (The Passion Translation) In other words, if you want a nice, clean, undisturbed church, that's fine. You can have one with no people in it. If you want an abundant harvest of people, it's probably going to be messy, and with more people comes more mess. And we need to be okay with that. If you want change, you need to be supportive of your pastors, working with them to develop the vision God has given them for the Church to impact your community for Christ. Working as a unified leadership team, you can prayerfully make the necessary changes, because without change, nothing is going to change.

Repeating Pete

So how do you go about developing a strong leadership team that can implement effective change? Let me tell you about a concept that changed my life, from a rough upbringing and leaving school at age 16 to developing successful companies. The transformation in me occurred when I heard about and adopted the Peter Principle. While I have written about the principle in previous books, I will reiterate it here because I believe its truths are profound. I hope never to stop embracing its wisdom. It applies to creating success in all areas, and definitely in developing churches and fulfilling the call of God on our life.

The Peter Principle, a concept coined by Laurence J Peter, states in essence that "We will progress in life to the level of our incompetence."[3] This means we can't accomplish more in our lives if we don't have the understanding to get us there. The reason I'm not more successful in my marriage, my parenting, my finances, my health, my career, and my relationship with God is that my competency is lacking somewhere in these areas.

People ask questions like these all the time: why am I not getting promoted, why isn't our company growing, why isn't our church or ministry more successful? The answer to all of these and more is the Peter Principle. Perhaps I need to become more knowledgeable in an area, or maybe I need to work on self-control. Whatever it is, I will only advance in life to the level of my incompetence and not any further. The Bible says in Hosea 4:6, "my people are destroyed for lack of knowledge." (NKJV) I would add, it is not just knowing something but being able to apply it.

The Peter Principle applies to individuals, departments, businesses, organizations, and churches alike. Your individual achievement in life exactly reflects your competency level. And your church or organization is precisely the size the competence of leadership has structured it to be. Is that too direct? Remember, tough love. This is not just worldly competence; it also includes proficiency in hearing from and following the Holy Spirit.

That said, too many church leaders discount developing an understanding of the natural things that lead to a thriving organization. I believe the Holy Spirit, who is our guide and direction, gives us wisdom in practical matters as well as spiritual ones, to be used for the Church's success. Quite bluntly, one of the reasons our churches have not flourished is that we don't have the knowledge or understanding of how to implement things that will make them successful. In our example of flipping restaurants, the reason the turnarounds worked is that the specialist knew how to develop a team of people that understood how to fulfill their roles, and he implemented strategies for a successful outcome.

We will talk more about how to do this, but the main thing now is to start understanding that "Everything rises and falls on leadership." Leadership is not one person. It is a team of people with abilities working together to succeed. Our organizations will rise to the level of the combined incompetence of all the individuals participating in it. There has never been an organization that can sustain growth past the competence of the leadership, so it is up to us to start working with and supporting our leaders to increase our leadership competency.

Leadership Unity

On our journey to increase our competency, we should ask ourselves, how do we create a successful, unified leadership team? I wish I could give you a simple prescription to follow: "Drink this amazing potion mixed by the Holy Spirit and your leadership issues will be solved!" The truth is, addressing these problems takes continual prayer and listening for the Holy Spirit's wisdom and direction. It may include many tough questions and conversations, like whether we have just been playing church or do we want to be the thriving Body of Christ we were meant to be. Ideally, I would advocate hiring or recruiting a professional who could A) walk you through the process of setting up healthy, functioning teams around a vision, and B) develop a strategy to accomplish it, a two-fold plan that is continually immersed in prayer. While I do understand this option may not be in your budget, there are still ways to support leadership and implement necessary changes to experience growth on any budget.

It is my personal belief that a select group of people is called by God to be pastors and the heads of churches. Even though I am a pastor, I'm thankfully not the senior pastor with such a tremendous responsibility placed on me. Most of us are called to take our place with our pastors and support them by helping them bring about their God-given vision. Unfortunately, there is no cookie-cutter recipe for how this will look. Just remember that it is essential to have the right people at the helm, and leadership is ultimately a combination of many people working in unity to fulfill the vision.

Big and Small

We talk about the Peter Principle as the answer to business and organizational success, but it also pertains to individual areas and departments. The Peter Principle applies to us as individuals, to us leading a serving team, ministry team, as department leaders, and throughout the entire church or organization. Let's put the Peter Principle to work for us by developing and educating ourselves, and surrounding ourselves with other quality leaders to help us. Remember, we are the leader of our life, so the principle applies. If there is a group of leaders, it is relevant to the overall leadership team for the outcome of the organization, in that we will rise to the level of the combined leadership's incompetence.

We all have strengths and weaknesses. It is up to us to develop our strengths and manage our weaknesses by building leadership teams of people who possess the gifts we are lacking. I have a saying; the smartest person in the room knows they are not the smartest person and they empower the smartest people to be the smartest people. It is my goal to get the highest caliber leadership team in the room which raises our level of competence and leads us toward successful outcomes.

We know good leadership is at the core of a thriving church or organization because "Everything rises and falls on leadership." We also know that change is necessary but challenging and uncomfortable. In the next chapter we'll look at Jesus' counsel on what type of leadership is most effective. Jesus specifically gave His followers a directive on what type of leader to be. If we follow His guidance, we will have increased success for the Kingdom.

Chapter 4 Reflection Questions

1. How can we make our leadership team stronger?

2. Do we need coaching or help to raise our competency? What does that look like?

3. What steps are you going to take to raise your leadership competency?

4. How can you support your pastor or other church leadership?

5. What is your real attitude toward change? What changes can you see that need to be made in order to foster growth?

[1] https://en.wikipedia.org/wiki/List_of_books_by_John_C._Maxwell#cite_note-4 accessed 10/22/2018

[2] https://www.inc.com/jeff-haden/the-top-50-leadership-and-management-experts-mon.html accessed 10/22/2018

[3] https://en.wikipedia.org/wiki/Peter_principle accessed 10/15/2018

Chapter 5: Jesus Says…What?!?

Jesus' disciples had a hard time grasping His idea of leadership. One minute they were arguing over who would be the greatest among them, and the next they were confused why Jesus, their Master, was washing their feet (Mark 9:33-37, John 13:1-17). James and John even had their mother petition Jesus to allow her sons to sit at His left and right side in His Kingdom (Matthew 20:20-28). Talk about awkward. It's probably not the best career move to have your mom ask your boss to give you a promotion over your coworkers, and then have the news leak to those colleagues. As always, Jesus turned this uncomfortable situation into a profound teaching moment for all of them saying, "You know that the rulers of the Gentiles lord it over them, and those who are great exercise authority over them. Yet it shall not be so among you; but whoever desires to become great among you, let him be your servant. And whoever desires to be first among you, let him be your slave." (Matthew 20:25-27 NKJV) In summary, Jesus was promoting servant-leadership

The Servant as Leader

The concept of servant-leadership has been around for ages (at least since Jesus walked the earth) but has become increasingly popular in the last few decades. Robert K Greenleaf coined the phrase "servant-leadership" in his

1970 essay, *The Servant as Leader.* In that essay, Greenleaf says, "The servant-leader is a servant first...It begins with the natural feeling that one wants to serve, to serve first. Then conscious choice brings one to aspire to lead."

The essay goes on to explain that the servant-first leader is distinctly different from one who is leader-first, based on a leader-first's need for power or control. Greenleaf continues his point that there are varying degrees between the two extremes of leader-first and servant-first:

> The difference manifests itself in the care taken by the servant-first to make sure that other people's highest priority needs are being served. The best test, and difficult to administer, is: Do those served grow as persons? Do they, while being served, become healthier, wiser, freer, more autonomous, more likely themselves to become servants? And, what is the effect on the least privileged in society? Will they benefit or at least not be further deprived?
>
> A servant-leader focuses primarily on the growth and wellbeing of people and the communities to which they belong. While traditional leadership generally involves the accumulation and exercise of power by one at the "top of the pyramid," servant-leadership is different. The servant-leader shares power, puts the needs of others first, and helps people develop and perform as highly as possible.[1]

In more traditional forms of leadership, the focus is on the leader and their accomplishments. The viewpoint is to make their success, growth, visibility, status, etc. the top priority. In servant-leadership, our focus changes to the people we are leading. Are our followers growing as people? Are they becoming more successful, healthier, thriving? Are their family relationships, spiritual walks, peace, and finances better because of their association with us? A servant-leader's heart is to help their people grow and be successful. Regardless of our position in a church or business, when we put our pride aside and start serving others, growth takes place, both within us and the organization.

Followers Letterhead

Jesus' followers, including Paul, became great examples of servant-leadership, especially after His ascension into Heaven. They came a long way from fighting over who would be the greatest when they got to Heaven (Luke 9:46; Luke 22:24; Mark 10:35-45). The disciples' transformation can be seen in how they identified and referred to themselves within their letters. Let's look at how they described themselves on their "company letterhead."

After Jesus' ascension to Heaven, several of the apostles sent out letters to churches, and many of the books in the New Testament consist of these letters. Just like today, they had their title and "company" as the immediate reference at the top of their letterhead. Let's take a glance at how they referred to themselves as the immediate followers of Jesus, the apostles, and the "CEOs" of the Church.

Paul wrote most of the letters, or epistles as they're called, in the New Testament. The consistent humility that he shows in his letterhead is striking, considering his high level of education.

Romans 1:1—"Paul, a bondservant of Jesus Christ, called to be an apostle..."

1 and 2 Corinthians 1:1—"Paul, called to be an apostle of Jesus Christ..."

Galatians 1:1—"Paul, an apostle, not from men nor through man, but through Jesus Christ..."

Philippians 1:1—"Paul and Timothy, bondservants of Jesus Christ..."

Titus 1:1—"Paul, a bondservant of God..."

Examples of additional New Testament books that were letters written by other disciples include:

James 1:1—"James, a bondservant of God and of the Lord Jesus Christ..."

2 Peter 1:1—"Simon Peter, a bondservant and apostle of Jesus Christ..."

Jude 1:1—"Jude, a bondservant of Jesus Christ..."

So, what is a bondservant? Sounds pretty lowly to me. The definition of a bondservant is "one bound to service without wages" or "a slave."[2] I don't think the disciples used the word bondservant as just some first-century marketing ploy or tagline. "Hey, let's use 'Jesus' Bondservant' on our letterhead. It's very clever, catchy, and easy to remember." Introductions of letters are used to indicate the author's authority or position of prominence, assuring the reader that the contents of the letter are valid and credible. Aren't you more likely to take someone's advice regarding your medical issues when you see the letters M.D. on their letterhead? While some of the disciples were either well-educated or leaders of the Christian Church, they took the opposite approach when it came to giving themselves titles of self-importance. Instead, they pledged their permanent devotion to Jesus Christ as his "slave" (bondservant) and "messengers commissioned to carry out the instructions of the commissioning agent" (apostle), indicating that their authority came *solely* from the One whom they served.

Addressing the early church from this position of humility and dedication to Christ as servant-leaders sounds intriguing. The real-life results of the disciples representing themselves this way is that they would be martyred. This takes things to a much higher level of commitment. We were all called to lay down our lives to serve others (Matthew 20:26-28). Thankfully, for the majority of us, we will not be asked to literally die for others; however, we are asked to help them and minister to them (Matthew 20:26-28, 28:19).

Paul and many of the original disciples all came to the same conclusion for their title and job description: "We are bondservants of Christ and we are to serve Him by serving humanity." I believe this same thing carries over to us as leaders. We should stay in the position of being servant-leaders by helping others find answers to life problems, which is ultimately Jesus.

Church/Congress

I was talking with a pastor one day and I surprised him, and myself, with the random comment, "I think churches are like Congress." I'm sure he was wondering where in the world that comment came from and where the conversation was headed. I was curious myself. Backing up my thoughts, I explained that in the early stages of this country, we needed leadership to direct it. The United States' Founding Fathers put their lives on hold; they sacrificed their time and finances to come together and use their abilities and talents to serve the interests of the people they represented. While people like Thomas Jefferson and Alexander Hamilton had many differing opinions, they shared the goal of being free from British rule. These two, along with the other Framers, put their successful careers as military officers, lawyers, authors, clergymen, educators, and inventors on hold or secondary for the cause of freedom. Over the centuries, there was a gradual power and financial shift and the roles eventually reversed. The nation's leaders, who initially served the masses, gradually took the power and became the served—becoming paid government employees and some even accepting funds from lobbyists to vote a certain way on an issue. The shared goal is now often ignored for the sake of self-interest. An evening watching cable news or a brief search of political scandals that have plagued some of our elected representatives quickly confirms this change.

I think a similar thing has happened in many churches. At one time, men and women of God put everything on hold and put God first. They connected with people any way they could to tell them about Jesus and met anywhere, even in the face of persecution, to hear His teachings. The Body of Christ took Jesus' words about "loving your neighbor as yourself" seriously (Mark 12:31). There are remarkable stories about the Early Church and their role in rescuing orphans, caring for those afflicted by deadly plagues, often losing their lives in the process. The self-sacrificial nature of early Christians and their devotion to meeting others' needs amid miserable circumstances had an enormous effect on the growth of Christianity in the first few centuries after Christ's death.

Over time the Church function has inverted, and in many congregations it may appear that we exist to serve church leaders or ourselves, and not the community at large.

Entitlement Excuses

Some church leaders may be thinking, "Mac, people expect too much from the Church nowadays. If the pastor doesn't personally greet a guest, invite them to lunch, and take their suggestions for the next sermon, they leave. People are just too entitled!"

I'm not saying that we need to fulfill every demand or suggestion from anyone who walks through our church doors. However, if you will recall, we spent a great deal of time talking about the basic premise of growing a business or church—meeting needs—and that if we are going to increase and influence people, we have got to get good at it. What I am saying is that mature members of the Body of Christ have got to look outside of ourselves and what *we* need (or may feel entitled to), discern the difference between people's needs and wants, and then focus on serving others as the Holy Spirit gives us wisdom.

As a leader, I can't change society's inclination toward feeling entitled. They can feel that way all they want. I can only change my attitude and how I serve them. That doesn't mean I cater to their entitlement mentality; I need to help them out of that mindset into something bigger. As a servant-leader, it is my responsibility to serve, set an example, and create a vision so great that they will want to grow out of their entitlement tendencies and become servant-leaders also.

Jesus was the greatest servant, and He said that "if we are to be great we need to be a servant of all." (Matthew

20:25) It is amazing what just a couple degrees of change can do over a period of time to get us off course. The good news is that the same small course correction can get us back on track, changing lives for the Kingdom.

The Serving Principle

In the last few decades, it has become a more accepted truth that to achieve success in any organization, leaders need to operate from a position of servant-leadership. I recently read an article from a leading business publication with a subsection, "The 15 Best and Most Popular Servant Leadership Books of All-Time[3]." This article is a massive reflection on how widely accepted this principle has become by successful organizations in the business community.

They don't just talk about one random book on servant-leadership. The narrative on servant-leadership is so extensive and consists of so much data that there is a multitude of articles, books, podcasts, and videos on the subject. The list of resources is so vast that they had to limit their results to the top 15 best books on the subject. Is it strange that the business world is better at articulating and operating in servant-leadership than the Church? Jesus was the greatest example of servant-leadership! During the era Jesus was on earth, this idea was completely contrary to the societal norm of ruler/subject relationships.

Jesus' teaching at that time would not have been considered just controversial; it would have been considered totally outrageous and potentially very dangerous. I can hear the disciples muttering, "Last week He told us to 'drink His blood and eat His flesh;' this week He tells us that 'leaders should serve their followers.'

(John 6:53-56, Matthew 20:25) Is this opposite day or has this guy been wandering around in the hot desert too long?"

Servant-leadership starts with the basic concept that the leader should serve others to a better outcome. As a servant-leader, I should be interested in all areas of wellbeing for my staff or followers. If I'm serving them, they should be healthier and accomplishing more under my leadership or I'm doing something wrong. There are many characteristics of a servant-leader, but the foundation of it is caring for the people we are leading. If we love people, we want them to excel and thrive in all areas of their lives. We want people to be better off because they are connected to us. While this may sound like it only applies to those in positions of power in a local church (i.e., the pastor, department heads, elders, etc.), this is not the case. If we are followers of Jesus, we are called to servanthood. Everyone influences someone, and thus we can all endeavor to cultivate the attitude of a servant-leader in our own lives.

Here are some attributes of a servant-leader. Some of them may apply more to those in an official leadership capacity, but we can broadly apply the general principles in our day-to-day interactions with others.

1. **Really care about your people.** People go through many real-life situations with health, marriage, kids, finances, etc. Most of these things are outside of the business environment, but they affect the individual's wellbeing. Care about the individual personally, not just about their production.

2. **Communicate**: It is up to us as leaders to share a vision and communicate with our followers. I have a saying, "I know you can't read my mind, so I need to communicate." Understand, I can't read your mind either, so you have to keep me posted on what is going on in your mind and life. As servant-leaders, we must communicate. No excuses.

3. **Know the condition of your flock**: I have an open-door office policy, which means my office is always open for staff to stop by if they have an urgent situation, unless I'm in a private meeting or on a private phone call. Our team knows that if they need to talk to me, I'm available. While organizational size can impact this (or we fall into the Moses trap of being everything to everyone), my main staff members have my cellphone number, and I'm always available to them in times of need. I have been phoned at 3 AM when there has been a family tragedy, and I was okay with taking their call because I knew it had to be important. I know we need to have boundaries, but most people don't take advantage of this. If they need me, I'm available. That is the commitment I made to them when they became part of our organization, and it is my responsibility to them as a servant-leader. As part of knowing the condition of the flock, I walk around and check in regularly with most staff to see how they are doing. I like running into them and just doing a quick update to sense how things are going in their lives. Are you available to the people who you influence? Do they have the sense that they can reach out to you during a time

of crisis, or do you give off the vibe that you would rather not be bothered?

4. **Listen**: When I check in with our team, I'm listening with both my ears and heart to sense how they are doing. How is their family doing? Any stresses in their life I should know about? How are we at listening to others? This skill also applies to our friends and family, not just those we might mentor or lead at church.

5. **Encourage**: Most of us could do much better in the encouragement and appreciation department. Statistics indicate that one of the main reasons people leave a job is that they do not feel encouraged or appreciated by leadership.[4] One reason people don't praise is the wrong belief that "If I encourage them, they will think that they are doing a good job and will not try as hard." Instead, some in leadership positions withhold appreciation and use criticism like a stick to indicate that people never quite measure up to expectations. This is probably a more significant reflection on the leader's need for growth, rather than the follower's poor performance. While there should be a level of expectation and accountability, this should be balanced with encouragement and appreciation to produce lasting positive results.

6. **Stewardship**: As a servant-leader, I want to be a good steward of the time and abilities of the people God sends me. I despise having to do busy work—what a waste of valuable time! So, out of

respect for our people, I don't want them to have to do busy work either. "We have always done this report, but it has no purpose, except to sit in a folder." Sound familiar? That mentality is mundane and unproductive. If I have not shown value for the work, it is my fault. If there is no value in the work, let's eliminate it.

7. **Growth**: We need to continue to mentor people and help them grow so they can advance in their talents, passions, and job position. As a servant-leader, it is my responsibility to move people into areas where they will be the most productive for their personality and skill set. In some instances, this has meant that in their best interest, I need to move a high-achieving individual to another church or company. What is best for the individual to accomplish their long-term goals and the burning desires within them? I like to ask employees, "What has God placed in your heart to do or be and how can I help you achieve it?" I then become a coach. "What steps do you need to take to accomplish that goal?" As their life changes and develops, it is my commitment to help them in this journey. Regardless of whether we lead people at work, at church, or in our personal life we can always encourage others' growth and development, cheerleading them to accomplish their dreams.

As a servant-leader, it is normal for me to ask staff or others at the end of meetings, "How can I help you? What can I do for you to help you accomplish what you are trying to do?" The Israelites were told to make bricks and then they weren't given any straw, which is the main ingredient for a good brick (Exodus 5:7). If I don't want to come across like a tyrannical Egyptian Pharaoh, I need to find out what people need to accomplish our agreed-upon outcome and help them get it. It may not be practical to fulfill all their requests, but unless I ask the question, I can't help them with the answer. Maybe they need equipment, manpower, more advanced notice, money, time, etc. Unless I, as the servant-leader, help them solve what they think is stopping them from accomplishing the goal, how can I expect them to achieve the outcome? I might be the very reason these people are not reaching their goals. Maybe they need information, a decision from me, or perhaps clarification. It is possible that I am the obstacle preventing them from moving forward and at the same time I'm demanding, "Where are the bricks you are supposed to be making?"

Real Life

When I first started in business, I was not yet a Christian and very selfish. Life was all about me and what I could attain. Later, through the influence of Christian businesspeople, I accepted Jesus as my Savior. Through their mentoring, my viewpoints on leadership gradually changed.

As Mac is a little uncomfortable telling you what a great servant-leader he is, I'm stepping in to write this section. This is Jenny, his assistant of over 16 years. Much of what I know about business, perseverance, loyalty, and unwavering faith, I have learned from Mac. Does it seem strange to say that about a boss? I hope not, because in some ways, that is the essence of servant-leadership. While I am very much his employee, he has always cared far more about my family (as well as those of my coworkers) and me than he did about the task at hand. Yes, he has always had high expectations of us, we work hard, and we get a lot done. One of my coworkers even commented that he is the most demanding person she has ever worked for, but also the easiest person in the world to work for. How is that possible? It is the way he conducts himself toward us. It is the fact that I never leave a conversation with him without being asked, "What can I do to help, or what do you need from me?"

As you can imagine, in the last 16 years a lot of real life has happened. He has celebrated my getting married, the birth of my two children, and has made every effort to allow me to continue working for him while taking on the responsibility of raising a family. During a significant downturn in the economy, which had a considerable impact on one of his companies, he stopped taking a paycheck for months to make sure that the rest of us were provided for and could still feed our families. Speaking for all of his employees, he has mourned with us in the death of family members; stepped in with extra finances when something unexpected came up; paid for additional education, books, and software when that's what we felt we needed to do our jobs; been a close confidante in times of crisis; and a constant prayer warrior. Our work is never about making Mac look great; it is always about working together to accomplish the vision that he has set before us.

Hey, it's Mac again, with another story that exemplifies servant-leadership. I was driving to the house of a successful business friend of mine and on the way I passed an incredible, ornate, multi-story brick home in the same subdivision that was under construction. When I got to my friend's house, I asked him who was building the amazing home down the street. His reply was, "Oh, that's one of the foremen at our company." That mentality always stuck with me. I think that is how we should be, and maybe how God sees us. "Hey, see that person who is debt-free, generous, and prospering? That is one of My Kingdom children." When people see our staff, hopefully they see a team that is prospering financially, personally, and spiritually. That is the result of real servant-leadership.

Servant Companies

In the corporate world, some of the most successful companies have a culture of servant-leadership. Here is a list of some companies that reportedly use the philosophy of servant-leadership: Marriott International, Starbucks, 7-11, Zappos.com, Pizza Hut, Southwest Airlines, Toro Company, AFLAC, Nordstrom, Men's Wearhouse, Service Masters, Herman Miller, the Container Store, and Chick-Fil-A.[5] Speaking of Chick-Fil-A, I was at a national conference of John Maxwell Coaches, and one of the speakers was Dan Cathy, son of Truett Cathy, the founder of Chick-Fil-A. Dan Cathy is known as an amazing servant-leader. When he comes to corporate headquarters, he reportedly parks as far as he can from the front entrance so he can save the closer parking spots for employees, and he picks up garbage in the parking lot on his walk to the front door. The day I heard him speak at the conference, Cathy had gone out for his daily run, which strategically went to a Chick-Fil-A restaurant. He picked up garbage in the parking lot before entering to help clean tables and once again taking out the trash before leaving to run back to his hotel.

On a side note, at the same massive facility we were having our conference, there was also a conference for Chick-Fil-A franchise owners. What was interesting to me was the incredible high-quality people attending and how polite and accommodating they were to other patrons of the hotel. Here was a chance for these franchise owners to get out of their communities, away from their business, relax, and have a good time. However, around the pool and throughout the lobby, these individuals were continually seen serving and blessing others. The apple doesn't fall far from the tree. I commend the Chick-Fil-A founders and franchisee owners. Our company founder and CEO is King Jesus, how are we doing following his example of servant-leadership?

Inverse Hierarchy of Leadership

My mentors also taught me that the customer was ultimately our real boss, and it was in our best interest to serve them if we wanted to be successful and prosper. The better we figured out how to serve the most people, the more successful we would be. This same thing applies in the Church. If we are focused on helping our community and congregation, it will make our church a raving success. One viewpoint of leadership is the triangle, with the CEO/head honcho at the top and layers of leadership cascading down with vice-presidents, managers, supervisors, down to the "lowly" laborers. When it comes to the Church, the inverse of the triangle is far more accurate. Jesus was the ultimate servant-leader, and He gave His life so all of humanity could be better off. This form of leadership continues with all of us called to be servant-leaders to the people in our sphere of influence.

Jesus gave us His leadership directive when he said "... whoever desires to become great among you let him be your servant." (Matthew 20:26 NKJV) The Church still seems to get confused by this concept. If our total focus is on how we can serve the members of our congregation and our community, how can we not be growing? You're right; this makes absolutely no sense! We are so busy thinking about our church-growth agenda and how we want others to fit into those plans that we aren't helping people with their needs. Can you imagine any business being successful with this approach? If I was determined to do my business this way, the number of people I was able to relate to would be greatly reduced. However, this is exactly how many churches proceed. The attitude seems to be, "This is how we do it here, and if you don't like it, something is wrong with you." If my real intention is to serve others, I need to find out what their actual needs are and do my best to help them.

While the concept of servant-leadership has been around at least since Jesus walked the earth, it was dramatically reinforced to me one evening when the Holy Spirit asked me three thought-provoking and revolutionary questions which we will cover in the next chapter. These questions have changed my life, and I hope they will change yours.

Chapter 5 Reflection Questions

1. How can you implement the concept of servant-leadership in your life?

2. What are some ways that you can improve your communication with those around you?

3. How can you get better at appreciating and encouraging your followers?

[1] https://www.greenleaf.org/what-is-servant-leadership/ accessed 02/08/2019

[2] https://www.merriam-webster.com/dictionary/bond%20servant accessed 04/17/2019

[3] https://www.inc.com/marcel-schwantes/15-best-servant-leadership-books-of-all-time-to-read-before-you-die.html accessed 09/02/2019

[4] https://www.forbes.com/sites/lizryan/2018/04/17/the-top-ten-reasons-great-employees-quit/#618094581cd5 accessed 02/11/2019

[5] https://www.modernservantleader.com/featured/servant-leadership-companies-list/ accessed 04/08/2019

Chapter 6: Three Questions from the Holy Spirit

As you can probably tell, I'm always trying to whittle down concepts and ideas to a base key element. Once I figure out the precept, it becomes a guiding principle in my life. Some of those maxims I have shared are, "Everything rises and falls on leadership," and "We should be servant-leaders." Years ago, I had a core question: "What is the one thing that all of us could achieve that would fully encapsulate a successful Christian life from Heaven's point of view? From the Father's perspective, what is the one accomplishment that shows you have succeeded at what you were put on earth to do?"

Most people wander through life with no real end goal or result that they can weigh their decisions against. In my 30s, I figured out the saying, "He that dies with the most toys wins," is a terrible motto to live by. However, many people devote their entire life to the pursuit of worthless trinkets. Some would say being saved and going to Heaven is the end goal. While I know that is extremely important, I'm not sure that should be the ultimate achievement of our lives because what would our motivation be after we have accepted Jesus as our personal Savior? After coming to this conclusion, that's when the Holy Spirit lead me to the story in Matthew 25, the Parable of the Talents.

In my last book, *Well Done, Finding and Fulfilling the Call of God on Your Life,* I recount a turning point in my life. In it, I tell the full story of preparing a sermon for church when I had a profound experience in which I heard the Holy Spirit tell me I should preach on the Parable of the Talents. The Holy Spirit indicated I should warn people that this was very serious, and we should not be wasting our lives on worldly pursuits and inconsequential things like collecting the most toys or conquering the most recent video game. We are ultimately going to be held accountable for our life and the gifts and abilities we were given. Since this book is an extension of that concept, let's quickly recount the Parable of the Talents and see how it applies to churches fulfilling the call of God.

The Parable of the Talents

The parable is found in Matthew 25:14-30 (NKJV), and I have typed it out not only for your convenience, but to show how immensely important it should be to all who call themselves followers of Jesus Christ.

> 14 "For *the kingdom of heaven is* like a man travel-
> ing to a far country, *who* called his own servants
> and delivered his goods to them. 15 And to one
> he gave five talents, to another two, and to an-
> other one, to each according to his own ability;
> and immediately he went on a journey. 16 Then he
> who had received the five talents went and trad-
> ed with them, and made another five talents. 17
> And likewise he who *had received* two gained two
> more also. 18 But he who had received one went
> and dug in the ground, and hid his lord's money. 19
> After a long time the lord of those servants came
> and settled accounts with them.

[20] "So he who had received five talents came and
brought five other talents, saying, 'Lord, you delivered to me five talents; look, I have gained five
more talents besides them.' [21] His lord said to him,
'Well done, good and faithful servant; you were
faithful over a few things, I will make you ruler
over many things. Enter into the joy of your lord.' [22]
He also who had received two talents came and
said, 'Lord, you delivered to me two talents; look,
I have gained two more talents besides them.' [23]
His lord said to him, 'Well done, good and faithful
servant; you have been faithful over a few things,
I will make you ruler over many things. Enter into
the joy of your lord.'

[24] "Then he who had received the one talent came
and said, 'Lord, I knew you to be a hard man,
reaping where you have not sown, and gathering where you have not scattered seed. [25] And I
was afraid, and went and hid your talent in the
ground. Look, *there* you have *what is* yours.'

[26] "But his lord answered and said to him, 'You
wicked and lazy servant, you knew that I reap
where I have not sown, and gather where I have
not scattered seed. [27] So you ought to have depos-
ited my money with the bankers, and at my coming I would have received back my own with interest. [28] Therefore take the talent from him, and give
it to him who has ten talents.

[29] "For to everyone who has, more will be given,
and he will have abundance; but from him who

does not have, even what he has will be taken away. [30] And cast the unprofitable servant into the outer darkness. There will be weeping and gnashing of teeth."

The Parable of the Talents from a Business Point of View

The Parable of the Talents is all about stewardship. What are we doing with what we have been given? Two factors tell us we should pay special attention to this parable. First off, the fact that Jesus is teaching the parable elevates its level of importance. Second, it is an accepted interpretation that Jesus is speaking about Himself within it. That right there tells us we need to listen carefully. The beginning of the parable is immensely powerful as Jesus starts with the foundational statement, "For the Kingdom of Heaven is like..." I really believe most of us gloss over this truth way too quickly. Jesus is almost blowing a trumpet as He stands before his followers and He says, "Hey, listen up! I'm going to teach you a profound truth, and the truth is, *This is what the Kingdom of Heaven is like!*" Pause and internalize what Jesus is saying; get ready to absorb the amazing insight He is about to present. The Parable of the Talents—this is what the Kingdom of Heaven is actually like! And buckle up, because it has huge ramifications when it comes to the growth of the Church.

Parable Recap

In the parable, the Master (commonly inferred to be Jesus) goes away to a far country. Before He leaves, He gives His three servants (followers) talents based on their abilities and tells them He will be back at an unknown time to see how they stewarded His abilities. This story is such a direct parallel to what the Bible says regarding Jesus and His return to earth, and we, as His stewards, either overlook or refuse to accept responsibility for our role in this scenario as we await His Second Coming. Servant Number One gets five talents, and this servant doubles that to ten. The Master tells him, "Well done, thou good and faithful servant." Servant Number Two gets two talents, gaining another two and also hearing approval with the phrase, "Well done, thou good and faithful servant." Servant Number Three takes a passive approach and doesn't use the talents the Master gave him, rather burying them instead.

How many of us are guilty of that? Unfortunately for Servant Number Three, he receives a powerful rebuke. The Lord says, "You wicked and lazy servant..." and casts the unprofitable servant into the outer darkness. Once again, I'm not a Bible scholar, nor do I need to be one to figure out that I don't want to receive that response. I don't want us wasting our time focusing on the wrong thing, which is what happens to the third servant. Instead, we should be laser-focused on becoming Servant Number One or Servant Number Two and receive the "Well done" response.

Hopefully, we can agree that a worthy goal for every Christian to aspire to is to hear their Master say, "Well done, thou good and faithful servant." In fact, this should be our ultimate goal as a Christian. It just doesn't get any better than that for followers of Christ. Since this book's main topic is how churches can hear, "Well done," I want to bring pastors into the conversation.

Pastors "Well Done"

Pastor means "herdsman" or "shepherd." A pastor is our guide, the person we can count on to lead us successfully through this journey of life. Thank you, Lord, for pastors! I know without great pastors in my life, I would've been sunk. If we asked most pastors, "At the end of your life, when you stand before the judgment throne, do you think you will hear, 'Well done'?" Maybe I'm an optimist, but I'm hoping most would say, "Yes!" Perhaps they would even expand their response with, "I think I will. I was called to be a pastor. That is the gift on my life, and yes, I became a pastor and fulfilled the plan for my life. I could have done better, but I believe I will hear, 'Well done.'" Excellent! I like it when people fulfill the call of God on their life!

Now let's go back to the evening I previously mentioned, the life-altering experience when the Holy Spirit asked me three simple but profound questions regarding the subject of pastors hearing, "Well done." Get ready for some powerful Holy Spirit reflections.

Wake Up Call

That evening was just like most others; I was puttering around the house working on projects, nothing unusual. Since I get up most days around 5 AM to pray, write, and exercise, I usually try to go to bed around ten-ish. As usual, I went right to sleep, but at midnight I awoke, unable to go back to sleep like a light switch that couldn't be turned off. Can you say nap instead of a full night's sleep? I'm not a numerologist and I don't put effort into tracking that sort of thing, although I know God is really into numbers. Anyway, on the night of 9/10, going into the day of the 11th, at 12 AM suddenly I was wide awake! My first thought was, "Wow, that seems kind of early for the Holy Spirit to want to chat. Usually, He wakes me up closer to two or three in the morning." Also, I typically wake up gradually; this was instantaneous. You're awake! Little did

I know that over the course of the night I would be having a wonderful time with the Holy Spirit. I got up and moved to my home office where I could sit comfortably to pray. That's when He asked me the following three questions, which all pertained to pastors. Thankfully, I immediately texted them to myself so I wouldn't forget.

Question #1

I had a normal prayer time, and then at about 12:58 AM, a very clear question shot straight into my mind from what seemed like nowhere. The Holy Spirit asked, "Do you think pastors will hear, 'Well done,' if no one in their church does?" Awkward silence. First off, I don't think He asks questions because He doesn't know the answer. "Hey, Mac! I have been pondering this question, and I just wanted to get your thoughts on it." Probably not. The Holy Spirit is always trying to get me to think more deeply and clearly from Heaven's perspective. So how do you answer such a profound question? What do you think? Do you think a pastor will hear, "Well done," if no one in their congregation does? The way the Holy Spirit asked the question, it seems like the answer would be, "No."

I have subsequently asked the question to many pastors and leaders, and everyone had that same negative response. The consensus is since a pastor is responsible to lead his flock, and if no one gets to greener pastures and the ultimate success of "Well done," it seems like a gigantic problem and the result of misplaced efforts. We may think we will hear, "Well done," just because we have fulfilled the call of God on our life, but what about all the people who are following us? If everyone under our stewardship fails and doesn't hear, "Well done," how well did we do as their leader? Once again, what do you think? Pause a moment and internalize this question. Will pastors hear, "Well done," according to Matthew 25 if no one in their congregation does?

After this revelation, I spent the next hour or so praising God for the compelling question. I reflected on it and just enjoyed my time with the Holy Spirit.

Question #2

Later in the morning, the same voice rocketed through my brain with the next question. This time, the Holy Spirit brought me His thoughts and input on church growth—a valuable addition to this book considering its topic. In the second question, He asked me, "If the pastor of a church of twenty-five people helped all of his church members move forward to hear, 'Well done,' would the church stay at twenty-five?" Wow, once again immensely powerful. What do you think? If a pastor is a true servant-leader and devotes his energy to helping each member of his congregation to succeed in the calling on their life and hear, "Well done," will the church stay the same size?

This was another question containing amazing clarity and common sense. It seems impossible to help people in our congregation succeed in hearing, "Well done," and our congregation *not* increase. However, this would create a chain reaction and another problem because we would have more new people. If we also helped those people hear, "Well done," it would grow even more and then the cycle would repeat. Then we would be asking what to do with all the new people attending our churches. I guess some problems are better to solve than others.

Question #3

I spent the early morning hours praying, praising God, and reflecting on what I was learning. One more time, the

Holy Spirit rattled me, this time with a question concerning what the servants did with the talents they were given in the Parable of the Talents. For the last question, He asked, "What if the talents inside the people attending each church were the talents the pastors were given and would be held responsible for?" Instantly I knew what the Holy Spirit meant. When I thought of the gravity of the question, I was overwhelmed by its significance. We know pastors are stewards and responsible for their flock, from a Biblical standpoint, what if the people in a pastor's church held the talents he was actually given and would be held responsible for? Breaking it down even further: what if pastors are responsible as stewards of the talents of their flock, thus held accountable for the stewardship of all the talents their flock possesses?

Suddenly, I wasn't sure I really wanted to be a pastor. The enormity of a pastor's responsibility for his flock took on a whole new level of accountability. The Holy Spirit's questions are what I call a critical moment of insight. If we, as pastors, actually believed the people we are entrusted with housed the talents we were going to be accountable for, would we continue to do church the same way? There is another ramification of the question though. It implies the people and their exact talents were specifically placed inside each pastor's church—for the benefit of the pastor, the church, and the Body of Christ. After that night, the seriousness of helping pastors and their congregations hear, "Well done," has taken on a new significance for me.

Years ago when the Holy Spirit first talked with me about people hearing, "Well done," He did it in the form of an admonition. "Mac, warn people not to waste their lives in worldly pursuits." I think this third question is also a warning to us, as pastors. "What are you doing with the flock I entrusted to you?"

To make sure we retain this crucial information, let's revisit the insights of the evening. "Well done" is the ultimate achievement Christians can attain, because it represents that we accomplished exactly what the Master designed us to do. We, as pastors, will be held accountable for our teaching, and because we are called to be servant-leaders, we should put a priority on helping our people hear, "Well done." If we help the people in our church hear, "Well done," our churches will grow because we are releasing the Master's talents and abilities He placed in them for their stewardship and success. As pastors, part of the actual talents we have been given are housed in the people who are sitting in our churches. It is our responsibility to serve and help them for Kingdom success.

Serve to "Well Done"

I believe the Holy Spirit revealed these questions to me so I could pass them along, leading each of us to become more introspective about our leadership roles and more effective for the Kingdom of God. We should be questioning how well we are ultimately functioning as a servant-leader if we do not help the people God entrusted to us to be successful and hear, "Well done." As leaders, would we hear, "Well done," ourselves if we did not help and serve our flock, the ones placed in our care, to achieve what God has called them to do?

As church leaders, our focus should be on serving others to their success. Let's spend our time praying, seeking God, serving, equipping, and empowering our congregation to help them accomplish what God has called them to do for the Kingdom. What if we took the Parable of the Talents in Matthew 25 seriously and our whole agenda was: "We are serving you, and we want to help as many of you as possible fulfill the call of God on your life, and hear Jesus say, "Well done." We want to help you discover your gifts and abilities and then help you use them for maximum Kingdom return. The vision of our church is large, and we want to help as many people as we can discover, develop, and use their abilities as part of the Body of Christ. We are servant-leaders, and we are here to serve God by serving you for ultimate Kingdom success." If we do these things, will we have to worry about church growth? I believe that if we are good stewards of His people, He will continue to bless us with more people and overall church growth.

I know many of you pastors are probably thinking, "I want my church to grow—that's why I'm reading this book—but building a church takes a lot of extra work! There goes the little free time I had left." As a fellow pastor, boy, can I empathize with you. However, what if that wasn't the case? What if we have been misunderstanding the pastor's job description all along? Let's find out as we continue this journey together.

Chapter 6 Reflection Questions

1. What are your reflections on the three Holy Spirit questions?

2. How are you stewarding your talents? How are you stewarding the talents of those under or around you?

3. How are you going to help ensure the words "Well done," are heard by the people around you?

Chapter 7: Open a Can of God Pod

As each one has received a gift, minister it to one another, as good stewards of the manifold grace of God (1 Peter 4:10 NKJV).

Called Not to Minister

I'm not a theologian, heck, I don't even play one on TV; however, the Holy Spirit's three questions made me wonder what the Bible says pastors are actually supposed to be doing. As I stated at the end of the last chapter, I believe the Holy Spirit's questions indicate we, as church leaders, have a responsibility to help our people hear, "Well done," by developing their talents and putting them to use for the Kingdom.

Unfortunately, that is not how most churches function. Growing up, I always believed that ministry was to be done by the people God had called to do it, namely pastors. Heads up! It's homework time. Let's check to see what the Bible really says. The book of Ephesians talks about the positions of apostles, prophets, evangelists, pastors, and teachers and gives some guidance on their job descriptions. Let's look at this passage with a teachable heart because our preconceptions of what pastors are supposed to do could be significantly limiting what God does through ***all*** of us.

In Ephesians 4:11-12 it says, "And [God] Himself gave some to be apostles, some prophets, some evangelists, and some pastors and teachers, for the equipping of the saints for the work of ministry, for the edifying of the body of Christ" (NKJV). "Equip" means "to supply with the necessary items for a particular purpose,"[1] or in other words, to get people ready for or to provide the necessary elements so they can do what they are called to do. According to dictionary.com, "minister" means "to perform the function of a religious minister, to give service, care, or aid, or to contribute, as to comfort or happiness."[2]

With or without a theology degree, I think most of us can agree that in this passage, "saints" are those who have dedicated themselves to the teachings of Jesus Christ (aka the Body of Christ), and that "the work of ministry" is serving in some capacity with an overall goal of bringing the Gospel of Jesus Christ to others.

It's interesting how many times I have read this verse over the years, and how I had never really taken the time to think about what it said. It was so ingrained in me that the apostles, prophets, evangelists, pastors, and teachers should be the ones who are doing all the ministry, that I completely missed what it was saying. In many churches, the expectation is that the pastor is the one responsible for all the hospital visits, marriage counseling, crisis intervention, leading our neighbor to the Lord, along with teaching a Sunday school class, leading a small group, and preaching Sunday mornings and Wednesday nights. Is it any wonder pastors have such a colossal burnout rate? Biblically this isn't their job description!

The Bible clearly gives the direction that these individuals are supposed to ***equip*** the rest of us for ministry. So, if I put these concepts together: the apostles, prophets, evangelists, pastors, and teachers should be supplying the Body of Christ with the necessary items (or getting them ready) to serve or care for others—with the overall goal of bringing the Gospel of Jesus Christ to them. The Bible says the rest of us are the ones who are supposed to ***do*** the work of the ministry. What a novel concept! So what does that mean in terms of helping our people hear, "Well done," and accomplishing our goal of church growth and maximum Kingdom results?

Church Change

As I have previously mentioned, I find it interesting that when I talk about church growth, some people have the mindset that it is all up to God. Their thought process goes like this: "We are praying, but it is God's church, and He is all-powerful, so if He wants the church to grow, He will bring in the people to do it."

Let me get this straight. God is sitting on His hands in Heaven while cults and service clubs are growing, but The Bride of Christ, His Beloved Church is not? It's like saying, "When God wants the house I live in to be clean, He will do it," or "When God wants me to lose weight, He will give me a desire to work out and eat healthy food." And of course, "When God wants my marriage to be better, He will change my spouse."

It sounds like we are the ones sitting on our hands and making religious excuses for not doing what we are supposed to do. This wrong thinking becomes the rationale for us not making the necessary decisions and changes to develop our churches the right way. Are there things we can do naturally and spiritually to help our churches grow? Of course!

Pirating Talents

If you haven't already guessed, I think there is a problem when civic groups grow faster than God's church. We may say God isn't involved in the growth of secular organizations like social clubs, businesses, or even cults; however, perhaps we are too quick in making this assumption. These organizations have regularly pirated the God-given abilities within people and used them for their advantage for decades, while many churches are left clueless when it comes to this concept. The crazy thing is that this principle is from the very heart of God and is at the core of the Ephesians 4 call to "equip the saints for ministry." Fasten your seatbelts, we are about to unpack a rarely discussed radical truth for growth that can change your church and bring incredible success.

Secular Pastors

Is it awkward when business leaders have done a better job at being pastors and servant-leaders than the Church has? Ephesians 4 has directions for church leaders, outlining their job description; yet, businesses have been more effective at discerning peoples' God-given gifts and helping them apply those to serving others' needs through secular channels. How embarrassing! Businesses know that if they are going to grow and succeed, they need the right people in the right positions, doing what they are gifted to do. Those that need salespeople have a process to identify that skillset, they hire those individuals, and then train them to put their talents to use for the organization's success. They know they need detailed bookkeepers, friendly receptionists, and talented people to handle the marketing and communications to the public. A business owner doesn't put an artist in accounting and an introverted bookworm in a cold-call sales position. That would spell disaster, misery, and a lot of wasted time and effort on the part of everyone. Perhaps the Church should clue in on this!

Anointed Sinners

In this conversation, just for discussion and reflective purposes, I think it is beneficial for us to talk about the example of an amazingly gifted person who didn't end up serving God to their full potential. When I think of someone with remarkable musical talent, the first person who comes to my mind is the late Whitney Houston. For those of you who are too young to know who Ms. Houston was—or you grew up in a cave—you can do a quick internet search and check out her incredible talent. Whitney's musical abilities were mind-blowing. While I think most of us would agree that she was extraordinarily gifted, I believe that her ability came from God. I don't know how such amazing talent could *not* be a gift from God. Remember, we were made in the image of God, and in the Parable of the Talents (Matthew 25), we were given the talents of the Master. So, I believe Houston had amazing talents from God, but she had the free will to decide what to do with them. I also think she had choices; some choices would move her closer to "Well done," and some wouldn't. At the age of 11, Houston started performing as a soloist in the junior gospel choir at the New Hope Baptist Church in Newark, NJ where she also learned to play the piano. Her first solo performance in the church was, "Guide Me, O Thou Great Jehovah."[3] Her talents were ultimately hijacked for ungodly outcomes, inhibiting her from accomplishing all she could with her life for God. Would Whitney have a following if she performed in a strip club and everyone was drunk? Yes. If she was walking with God, would you want her as part of your praise and worship team? This question could be a subtle IQ test. If you answer no to that question, I think this book could be a great help to you, and you may want to read it multiple times. Of course, we would all want Whitney Houston walking with God, and on our praise and worship team! She was made in the image of the Most High God, and like all of us, she had a choice regarding what she was going to do with her abilities. I'm not saying Whitney's ultimate calling was to sing at a church. I'm saying, like her, we all have giftings from God and we should be asking the Holy Spirit where He wants us to utilize our abilities for the most Kingdom benefit. So what does this have to do with church growth?

A God Pod

A seed pod is the protective cover that protects the enclosed seed. The seed holds the DNA of a mature plant. If the seed is nurtured and placed in a healthy environment, it will grow up to become what the Creator designed it to be, a healthy reproducing plant that is modeled after the original. We were made in the image of God and hold the identity of Christ. It is our responsibility to identify the attributes and talents of Christ on the inside of us and develop them for Kingdom purpose, so we resemble Christ.

Whitney Houston's singing ability was a gift placed inside her from God, and she had the option not to use the gift or use it at whatever venue she chose. She was a steward of her gifts and talents. I'm not putting Whitney Houston down. We all have the same responsibility, and I'm sure we have all missed fully using our skills to their highest potential. I know I have. We are all gifted in some proportion with abilities by our Master, and it is up to us to use those endowments in a meaningful way. When we empower people to use their talents, we are releasing their God-given gifts and attributes into the situation.

We are all God Pods. We are capsules, and within us we hold part of the identity of Christ, the Anointed One. When we release our God-given abilities into our church, it brings God's anointing, favor, and blessings onto the scene. The more people that are empowered to use their abilities, the more of God is released into our situation, resulting in more success and growth. We have seen this happen when a gang leader who had success in recruiting and directing a gang for evil gets saved, matures, and then uses the same leadership ability and charisma to build the Kingdom of God.

Leader of the Gang

The life and work of Nicky Cruz are a powerful example of this. Born in Puerto Rico, the son of a satanic priest, whose mother practiced witchcraft, Cruz was regularly abused from a very young age. In his early teens, he was sent to live with an older brother in New York. He quickly got caught up in the gang violence prevalent in the city and rose through the ranks to become a leader of the Mau Maus, one of the most feared gangs in New York City. A psychiatrist pronounced him a hopeless case, destined for "prison, the electric chair, and Hell" but Jesus Christ radically transformed his life. He has spent the last nearly 60 years traveling the world and has spoken to tens of millions of people in inner cities, prisons, street corners, and stadiums. He is a best-selling author, with over 12 million copies of his biography, *Run Baby Run*, in print. Cruz continues his mission of international evangelism dedicated to reaching urban communities.[4] Now there is an increase in the right Kingdom!

While Cruz's story is incredibly dramatic, the same dynamic and increased influence can be at work in all of us. The more we all seek God to have His abilities flow through us in the right way and channel those abilities to increase the Kingdom of God, the more success we will experience. Success will come when we identify, develop, and release our God-identity pods, through the direction of the Holy Spirit, for Kingdom growth. When all of us use the God-given abilities that are bottled up inside of us to change lives for the Kingdom, powerful things happen.

Watching Scotty Grow

I recently listened to a podcast by Scott Harrison,[5] and it once again reflected the point I'm trying to make. Scott had a conservative Christian upbringing but rebelled against it. He was gifted in the area of sales and promotion and became a leading nightclub promoter in New York. I may be going out on a limb here, but if you make your living organizing parties for MTV, VH1, and Bacardi your core beliefs may not be promoting godly family values. For years he had unbelievable worldly success, driving a BMW, living in a luxurious apartment. But after a decade of living the fast life, he had an epiphany about his job and life overall. "I realized I was the most selfish, sycophantic and miserable human being," he recalled. "I was the worst person I knew."[6]

After spending two years as a volunteer photographer aboard a hospital ship with a humanitarian mission to Benin and then Liberia, West Africa, he came back to New York to start charity: water, an innovative non-profit that uses 100% of its donations to provide clean water to places around the world.

Scott has the amazing God-given gift of marketing and promotion. Once it was used to sell decadence and escapism. Now he is using it to fulfill Matthew 10:42[7] to provide millions of people with clean drinking water.[8]

Imagine God Pod Release

Let's imagine the results of groups of people being released to use their God-given abilities, focused on a vision for Kingdom results. A pastor, who is the head of his flock, sees the vision and direction from God to guide the congregation. People gifted with a variety of different talents link arms with the pastor around this shared vision to change lives. Administrative people support the vision, marketing people get the word out, communications people help keep the message clear and accurate, teachers are behind the scenes teaching and discipling future leaders with the vision to change lives. People with mercy are caring for and encouraging those who are hurting. People with the gift of hospitality are helping others feel welcome and loved. Decorators are beautifying and caring for the church so it is attractive and appealing, and happy, warm-hearted greeters radiate joy and love, welcoming new attendees to our churches.

Let me break this down a bit further for you, so you can get a clearer picture of how this works. Let's take one area, a greeter. Greeters are often someone's first impression of the church. The greeter in our example takes this calling seriously and is working at being a great steward of their abilities and position, serving the Master to their fullest potential. They are giving every ounce of prayer and effort they can for the church's success of impacting lives. This greeter is serious about being the best possible servant and steward of their position, so they naturally do a better job. They believe they were born for their present function in the Body of Christ, and they do it to the best of their ability.

The greeter spends hours in prayer, interceding for the people they are going to greet. They know that the people they meet could be going through a living hell in their personal lives, and the warm smile and handshake, maybe a hug and a kind, encouraging word could help them make it through. Since they want to be the best they can at their position, they are also watching videos, listening to podcasts, and studying how to remember names better, the proper way to greet and encourage people, maybe even innovative ideas to follow up with and bless new people. They might stop and pray with someone who is having a bad day or get their number and call them back later, possibly even visiting them. The list of what a "lowly greeter" could do is nearly endless, and the effects they have on our church can be profound. So, in reality, the greeter is in no way lowly or insignificant! They are crucial to the Kingdom of God. They are doing all these things with no one asking them; they are just trying to be faithful with their talents for the Master.

Now imagine this kind of passionate, focused energy multiplied throughout the entire greeters' team with everyone praying, growing, developing, and working in unity to be the best possible greeting team they can be, representing Christ to people attending. This mentality doesn't have to stop with greeters. Let's magnify this concept even further. What if the entire congregation of volunteers and staff took their serving and stewardship of their gifts just as seriously. These amazing people were all empowered to be the very best they can be, from parking lot attendants, ushers, greeters, musicians, janitors, children's ministry workers, audio/visual technicians, and the list goes on. All these people are committed to serving God by praying and bringing their very best to the King, as they serve and impact others. If we do these things it will be impossible—yes, I said impossible—for our church to stay small. People will be drawn to it and tell their friends to attend because we are releasing the very abilities of God and His favor into our church by opening all our God Pods!

Think of all these people knowing that they are fulfilling the call of God on their lives and also bringing God's abilities into the environment. Radiating with this purpose and dedication, these people will be drawn to fervently pray, not only for wisdom and favor for their particular area of responsibility in the church but for their pastor as well. Isn't that a pastor's dream come true?

Another Question

The moment I woke up this morning, a question shot into my mind. "Why aren't businesses coming to the Church for answers?" It was like the Holy Spirit had been waiting all night for me to wake up. He seemed to be thinking, "I can't wait until Mac wakes up. I'm going to give him something to think about." Pondering the question, I couldn't think of why businesses would come to the church for answers to any problems. What can we teach them? Then I thought about the God Pod concept and that we, as Christians, hold the identity and wisdom of God on the inside of us. Then it hit me! Holy Spirit, you are right; the Body of Christ should be the leaders of thought and innovation. The world *should* be coming to us for answers. Why aren't schools and placement companies coming to us saying, "You are the best at helping people succeed by identifying and developing their giftings. What is your secret?" Corporations should be coming to us saying, "Your people have an extraordinarily high level of servant-leadership. Teach us how you do it."

Why isn't the music industry following our lead saying, "Let's watch the innovative music that churches are creating. We know their music will captivate the youth. We need to copy Christian artists if we have a chance of staying in business." Why aren't government agencies coming to us saying, "Your drug treatment programs are incredible! Everyone gets delivered of their addictions and becomes functioning members of society. How are you doing it? How are your programs so economical, efficient and successful? People are getting jobs, becoming productive, and now are *paying* taxes instead of costing taxpayers' money." We are the holders of the identity and giftings of Christ; so instead of the Church being irrelevant, why isn't there a reverse shift where the world is coming to *us* for answers?

God Pod Conclusion

Now we can see the advantage of serving our people to hear, "Well done." When we are true servant-leaders and emphasize helping our congregation use their God-given abilities, we are actually bringing more of God into our situation. This will ultimately cause our church to thrive and succeed in an incredible way.

It's one thing to see the importance of releasing the God-given abilities of people, but how do we do it? The next success principle for growth is one that Moses was directed to use. Just as it produced incredible results for him, it will also help us successfully release the God Pod abilities within people in our church.

Chapter 7 Reflection Questions

1. What are your reflections on Ephesians 4:11-12? How does it apply to you?

2. How would it change your effectiveness and impact if you focused on equipping others to minister?

3. Take a few minutes to imagine God Pod abilities released in your area of influence/ministry. What would that look like?

[1] https://en.oxforddictionaries.com/definition/equip accessed 04/10/2019

[2] https://www.dictionary.com/browse/ministering accessed 04/10/2019

[3] https://en.wikipedia.org/wiki/Whitney_Houston accessed

[4] https://nickycruz.org/wp-content/uploads/2018/05/Nicky_Cruz_Profile.pdf accessed 12/31/2018

[5] https://en.wikipedia.org/wiki/Scott_Harrison_(charity_founder) accessed 11/19/2018

[6] https://www.nytimes.com/2009/07/12/opinion/12kristof.html accessed 10/15/2018

[7] Matthew 10:42 42 And if anyone gives even a cup of cold water to one of these little ones who is my disciple, truly I tell you, that person will certainly not lose their reward." NIV

[8] https://my.charitywater.org/about/scott-harrison-story accessed 10/15/2018

Chapter 8: One Thing to Grow a Church

I was meeting with some pastors and was asked, "Mac, what is the one thing leadership should do to grow their church?" Talk about putting a person on the spot. "Hey, here is a pop quiz! Could you tell us just one thing that if every church did it, they would grow?" What would you say? What is the one thing needed to build a church? There are many great answers. Many people might say prayer or the presence of God, maybe a strong children's ministry, or small groups. How about miracles, healings, or amazing worship services? All these are definitely critical and necessary. My challenge with those as the definitive answer is that I have seen churches pray around the clock and churches that have these individual attributes; however, it does not necessarily mean they will grow consistently. I'm all for churches doing these things. I'm just not sure they are the one key factor. Once again, it is pointless to grow a church without prayer and the presence of God. Yes, part of the answer is leadership, because "Everything does rise and fall on leadership," but it goes deeper than that. What are those who lead the church doing?

Let's see what insight we can gain from Moses in the book of Exodus on how and why he changed his leadership style 180 degrees for a superior outcome.

Leadership Transformation

There are two main leadership styles, and we can see both at play in the book of Exodus. One of those styles works hand in hand with the God Pod concept—opening and utilizing people's God-given abilities for healthy organizational growth. The other tends to stifle growth and leads to a great deal of frustration. Let's take a moment and unpack the successful Biblical leadership style that can release the power of God Pods into your church or organization.

The transformation that Moses' leadership style underwent in Exodus 18 is very informative. First, let's review the back story. Moses is leading millions of Israelites on an extended camping trip, I mean, journey out of slavery in Egypt into a land God had promised His people. As is typical when you get two or more people together, there can be challenging situations and controversies. However, I can confidently say that most situations pale in comparison to a camping trip with millions of disgruntled people for ***forty years.*** Since Moses was held accountable for the people, and he may have read a very early pre-release version of John Maxwell's book and adopted the principle that "Everything rises and falls on leadership"—he took all of the responsibility on himself to hear from God for the Israelites' direction. Every day from sunup to sundown, day after day, people lined up before Moses so they could ask him questions and he would give guidance to them (Exodus 18:13-16). Pastors, does this sound more familiar? Thankfully his father-in-law stopped by; let's listen in on their conversation.

> [17] But Moses' father-in-law said to him (Moses), "This isn't the right way to do this. [18] It is too much

work for you to do alone. You cannot do this job by yourself. It wears you out. And it makes the people tired too. [19] Now, listen to me. Let me give you some advice. And I pray God will be with you. You should continue listening to the problems of the people. And you should continue to speak to God about these things. [20] You should explain God's laws and teachings to the people. Warn them not to break the laws. Tell them the right way to live and what they should do. [21] But you should also choose some of the people to be judges and leaders.

"Choose good men you can trust—men who respect God. Choose men who will not change their decisions for money. Make these men rulers over the people. There should be rulers over 1,000 people, 100 people, 50 people, and even over ten people. [22] Let these rulers judge the people. If there is a very important case, then they can come to you and let you decide what to do. But they can decide the other cases themselves. In this way, these men will share your work with you, and it will be easier for you to lead the people. [23] If you do this as God directs you, then you will be able to do your job without tiring yourself out. And the people can still have all their problems solved before they return home." (Exodus 18:17-23, ERV)

Two Leadership Styles

When we look at this Old Testament story, we see a reflection of two main styles of leadership. The first part of the chapter is command and control leadership: the leader at the top is expected to make all the decisions. Things change in verse 17 when Moses' father-in-law brings in some common sense and becomes an advocate for empowerment leadership. He says, "This isn't the right way to do this...It wears you out. And it makes the people tired." This blunt commentary cracks me up. Leave it to the Bible to hit you upside the head with a dose of reality: doing things from a position of control without empowering others to help wears you out, and it makes the people tired. Pastors, are you still tracking with me?

Instead, Moses' father-in-law gives the following instructions on how to step into empowerment leadership:

1. **Listen to the people.** Essentially, he is saying to know the condition of your flock and ask God what to do.

2. **Communicate and explain God's laws and teachings.** The people should have a set of godly guidelines or core values to live by that will help them make their decisions. What is interesting is at that time God had not given them the Ten Commandments; however, there was still a set of guidelines to follow.

3. **Choose some people to be judges and leaders.** And just in case you were confused about which people to choose for leadership positions, he cleared that up too. Make sure your leaders are godly men and women who live by these rules.

The passage says that following this leadership style will be mutually beneficial for both parties; it will lighten your load, and the people will have their issues solved. God wants us to be the solution to people's problems, and empowerment leadership is a key to do that.

Moses was instructed to establish layers of leaders to oversee the vast organization of travelers headed to the Promised Land. He learned from his father-in-law's directions how to effectively accomplish this, and so can we. Moses released the ability of wisdom for decision-making through these leaders. When it came time to build the tabernacle, he released men gifted explicitly in areas of all kinds of crafts to make the Tent of Meeting, the Ark of the Covenant, priestly garments, and all the other related furnishings (Exodus 31:1-11). Just as one of the greatest Biblical leaders learned how to walk in empowerment leadership, we should also endeavor to release the gifts of God on men and women, based on their God-given abilities to oversee levels of people and direct them by a set of guidelines.

Now that we have a general concept of the two main leadership styles, let's take a more in-depth look at them, comparing and contrasting their individual qualities.

Command and Control vs. Empowerment Mindset

Command and control is "a style of leadership that uses standards, procedures, and output statistics to regulate the organization. A command and control approach to leadership is authoritative in nature and uses a top-down approach, which fits well in bureaucratic organizations in which privilege and power are vested in senior management."[1]

Command and control leadership is based on maximum oversight which could be needed in circumstances of limited trust or facing very critical situations. This leadership is generally implemented because of some kind of fear. One possibility is that the leader fears people will make the wrong call, so everything must run through them, rather than teaching the people how to make decisions and giving them the latitude to take different paths to a satisfactory conclusion. In some cases, control leadership can even manifest through a passive-aggressive approach or outright avoidance with the intent to manipulate the situation. Another type of fear is a crisis that individuals are not skilled at handling. The leader must step in with a hands-on approach to make sure the organization survives and navigates through the situation. Our military generally operates under command and control, especially in combat. Decisions are made, orders are issued, and lives are saved as a result. In these types of circumstances, it is best if everything runs through central leadership for approval.

This authoritarian leadership can also manifest as micromanagement, in that it is expected that every task is performed precisely as the leader would do it. This can substantially limit creativity and flexibility, making things move much slower. With this mentality, the base question becomes, "What would the pastor or leader want me to do?" While this question seems right, it leads to an endless game of guesswork and hopeless mind-reading, resulting in inactivity as no one knows what to do.

The right questions should be: "How does this line up with our core values, mission, or vision statement? What is the best decision to make in this situation, based on those core values and the vision of where we are going?" When we have these key components as our true-north marker to navigate decision-making, it lowers the guesswork. This way, a whole team of people can approach an issue with a common viewpoint, rather than wasting time speculating based on analyzing someone's moods or whims. The number one attribute of command and control leadership is controlling people's behaviors by pointing out what is wrong. These leaders don't focus on what is working; they focus attention on the negatives, problems, and mistakes, and are happy to point them out.

Mistakes Can Be Good

Command and control leadership's modus operandi is to look for and find mistakes. Usually, the assumption is that mistakes are unacceptable, and they should be avoided whenever possible, thereby limiting innovation. Placing a high priority on not making errors can result in a culture where no one is willing to try anything new, which results in an organization that is stale and lifeless. Remember, if you ask the wrong question, you will get the wrong answer. If the underlying query is: "What would the leader have me do?" this will lead us to speculative and often wrong results. Again, the real question you should be asking is: "What is the best thing to do to arrive at our vision?" Another wrong question is: "What can I do so I won't get in trouble or be reprimanded?" The answer to that one is: "Do things the way we have always done it. Don't bring up any new, innovative ideas since they may not work, and you won't suffer the humiliating consequences." You may not be embarrassed, but you won't grow either.

As we learned earlier, control or ultra-micromanaging can come from a fear-based mentality. If I must micromanage every detail of my staff's activities, it could be because I don't trust them, or I think they will make mistakes. If I can't trust my team, I have either hired the wrong people, or I am leading incorrectly. If I am fearful that they will make mistakes, then that is another problem. What if we realized that the belief that mistakes are harmful could be wrong and understand the truth that they are useful and necessary for maturity and the growth process? Errors are natural and can be beneficial because they give us valuable feedback. Let's think of them from the standpoint that we are prototyping and creating a breakthrough invention. If we were trying new things, we would understand that missteps were natural and productive. They could be invaluable in the prototype process and lead us to brilliant results.

Let's take the batteries that we use every day for example. Thomas Edison numbered over 10,000 experiments with different chemicals and materials before he found something that worked. His friend and associate, Walter S. Mallory had the following to say about these experiments,

"[The research] had been going on more than five months, seven days a week, when I was called down to the laboratory to see [Edison]. I found him at a bench about three feet wide and twelve feet long, on which there were hundreds of little test cells that had been made up by his corps of chemists and experimenters. I then learned that he had thus made over nine thousand experiments in trying to devise this new type of storage battery, but had not produced a single thing that promised to solve the question. In view of this immense amount of thought and labor, my sympathy got the better of my judgment, and I said: 'Isn't it a shame that with the tremendous amount of work you have done you haven't been able to get any results?' Edison turned on me like a flash, and with a smile replied: 'Results! Why, man, I have gotten lots of results! I know several thousand things that won't work!'"[2]

No one would argue that these "mistakes" weren't vital in the invention of something that has a considerable impact on our daily lives.

Empowerment leaders understand that mistakes are profitable and necessary for progress. They give the leader feedback on what level their team is operating. If I know what errors my team is making, it gives me information about where they are and what they need to learn to move forward. I must clarify, there is a difference between an honest blunder and repeating the same wrong action over again due to laziness or apathy. I'm obviously talking about genuine mistakes. If we have a culture of perfection, where missteps are not acceptable, people will hide their errors, and we won't know their true capabilities or problems that exist. This is an unhealthy culture that will limit team improvement and success.

Not only do mistakes provide indispensable feedback, but they can also lead to significant innovation and breakthroughs. If you look through history, there is a long line of life-changing and even life-saving inventions that were the result of mistakes. A few of these include Penicillin, post-it notes, plastics, the pacemaker, the microwave, x-rays, anesthesia, Velcro, and let's not forget the Slinky, perhaps not life-changing, but certainly fun![3] Imagine how many millions of lives have been saved by some of these inventions that resulted from a mistake! Let's have the attitude that mistakes are beneficial and endeavor to learn from them, rather than avoiding them.

Celebrate for more

Let me give you another example of this shift in attitude toward mistakes. There is a business precept that asserts, "Whatever you celebrate, you will get more of." A key principle for a healthy empowered culture is to celebrate the attributes you want to increase. At an upcoming staff meeting, I knew we needed to have a great celebration with donuts and a very festive atmosphere. What were we celebrating? I wanted to celebrate the multitude of mistakes we had made at a welcome lunch for new attendees to our church. The event turned into a train wreck, stretching us way past what we knew how to do. I know you might be thinking, "Mac, you must have eaten lead paint chips as a child. Why would you ever celebrate mistakes? Won't you just get more of them?"

Actually, the thing I was celebrating was initiative. Up to that time, people were showing very little inventiveness. They had the viewpoint that everything needed to be perfect, which resulted in no one wanting to try anything new. The team had taken incredible steps to attempt something out of the box, and I wanted to reward and celebrate their initiative so they would continue to stretch. I commented, "It was awesome how many mistakes we made. It was like we set a new record for the number of blunders you can make at one time. Because of all the things we tried and the mistakes we made we are on the way to making this a very successful event. Congratulations on finding so many things we shouldn't do next month!"

I know God answers our prayer for guidance, and I know we pray and have the Holy Spirit's wisdom, but sometimes we need to make the necessary mistakes as quickly as we can to get the answers to our prayers. Think about what you want your culture to be and celebrate the attributes you wish to multiply in your organization.

Mistakes Are Not Equal

Just to clarify, I believe some errors, made with the right heart, are good and can have an ultimately positive outcome. The miscalculations I've talked about in the last two sections were all made in the context of moving ahead and making forward progress. We all know there are different types and magnitudes of mistakes. Not all are equal. Some mistakes can be celebrated. There are also real issues of character and decision-making that should lead to firing or legal proceedings. The very real consequence of empowerment is that we are responsible for our decisions.

I'm Empowered

As we give up the inclination to control every detail and become comfortable with allowing other people to make decisions, we're opening ourselves up to an empowerment culture. Empowerment means to give power or authority to; authorize, especially by legal or official means.[4] Empowerment is based on giving. In empowerment leadership, we look to give our followers freedom, authority, and decision-making capabilities around core values and a prescribed vision as their abilities develop. In this style of leadership, we try to provide more people decision-making authority, trusting in their abilities. The success of our endeavor compounds when people are empowered to release their God-given gifts and skills toward a common goal.

Jesus modeled empowerment leadership throughout His ministry. Here are just a few examples:

> He gathered His disciples together, told them to proclaim to others that "the kingdom of heaven has come near," and gave them the authority to drive out unclean spirits and heal sickness and disease (Matthew 10:1-8).
>
> He gave power over the enemy to the 72 that He had appointed to go out before Him into the towns (Luke 10:19).
>
> He gave His disciples the authority to spread the Gospel in the passage known as The Great Commission (Matthew 28:16-20).

Paul's relationship with Timothy and Titus, as well as the appointing of elders and deacons in the early church reveals a similar pattern of empowerment. (Acts 6:1-15, Titus 1:1-16, 1 Timothy 4:11-16).

Jesus allowed his disciples to make mistakes. With this information Jesus knew where His disciples were at mentally and what they were thinking, then he coached them. Think of Peter failing at walking on water (Matthew 14:28-33).

Empowerment is more art than science; thus, it is sometimes easier to explain in contrast to the more traditional command and control mindset. Though Jesus and the disciples modeled forms of empowerment leadership, most churches today are geared toward control. The guy at the top makes all the decisions. It is easy to see how they fall into this authoritarian leadership style because of the responsibility that the Bible places on the role of a teacher, warning that they will receive stricter judgment as they can lead people astray (James 3:1)[1]. When God makes pastors responsible for the spiritual health of their flock, it can easily put them in a defensive gatekeeper position. In these instances, nothing happens in the church without the pastor's input and approval. Pastors may also default to a control mentality because they have personally been betrayed or have heard devastating stories of some trusted charismatic confidante that had favor, then led many followers away, splitting the church and leaving the original pastor in a horrific mess.

Can this happen in an empowerment culture? It's possible, but not likely because the mindset and process of raising up leaders is entirely different. When our default is to walk in love, not fear, we open lines of communication and have conversations that we might not typically have. When people know we come from an empowerment perspective, they are more apt to share their goals and dreams because they see leadership as the people that God has selected to help them achieve their goals.

Let's see if this story sounds familiar to you. An associate pastor musters up the courage to share with his senior pastor that he feels led to start a church sometime in the future. The control-oriented pastor, not knowing what to do but concerned about a church split, acts out of fear and alienates the associate pastor. There is a significant amount of gossip, tension, and backbiting in the church because of the perceived friction between the pastors. Naturally, people start choosing sides. Afraid that he is losing control of his flock, the senior pastor ultimately forces the associate pastor out of the church. The associate pastor, following what he believes is God's leading, starts a new church. As things were so ugly and divided at the original church, a large number of people in the congregation feel disillusioned and quit church completely, while another group follows the associate pastor.

A church split, the very thing the senior pastor tried to avoid, has happened with a lot of devastated people in its wake.

What if the senior pastor's initial response had been one of love and empowerment?

Let's listen in on this same situation but from an empowerment perspective. "Associate Pastor Sid, thank you so much for sharing your heart with me about the desire God has placed within you to start a church. If that is where God is leading, I would be happy to spend more time training you, so your transition will be seamless. Also, there are a lot of valuable strategies and resources we have developed that you will need to be successful. We can provide them for you. They will help your new church thrive. Pastor Sid, I don't want you to be concerned about money or people. Before you leave, we will help train a team to go with you, and we will plan to help you financially. Let's communicate closely and work together to ensure that this dream God has placed in your heart is ultimately successful and many people are reached for the Kingdom!"

Which approach do you think will get better results, if we have an empowerment culture of open communication where we work arm in arm with Pastor Sid as he opens his church or if we oppose him? If we work against Sid, he won't feel comfortable openly telling us his plans. Instead, he will have to operate in secret to fulfill the call of God on his life. This is not good or healthy. Ultimately, if Associate Pastor Sid was called by God to open a church, I sure don't want to be the one that stands in his way. Eventually, I will be the one who must answer to God for becoming a stumbling block for him and the many others who were hurt by the church division. That's not a conversation I want to have with Almighty God. Ouch!

Gut Check

Here is a way we can tell which leadership mindset we are coming from: if we hear a person's thoughts or dreams to move forward and our first reaction is that we feel threatened, we are leading from command and control. If when we hear their desires to move forward and we start thinking of ways to help them, we are servant-leaders trying to empower them to succeed.

The following table is a snapshot of the difference between an empowerment and a command and control mindset to leadership.

Command & Control vs. Empowerment Leadership

Concept	Command & Control	Empowerment
Leads from	Front/Directs	Beside/Inspires
Viewpoint	Leadership knows best	Releases others' abilities
Staff Hierarchy	Subordinates	Colleagues
Supervision	Control/Micromanage-ment	Trust & delegation/ Self-management
Direction/Decision-Making Process	Tell what to do/What would the boss have us do?	Initiative toward stat-ed vision/What will get us to our stated result?
Mindset/Assessment	Right or wrong	Working vs. not working
Action	Permission-Based	Progression-Oriented
Mistakes are…	Bad	Necessary
Priority	Operations	Strategy
Communication	Need to know/Secrecy	Open Dialogue
Attitude	Condemnation/Fault	Encouragement

Maybe Empowered

When I talk with pastors and church leaders about empowerment, I get several different responses. The most common reply is that the senior pastor feels like they have some attributes of an empowerment organization; however, when I talk with the staff, they are not on the same wavelength and feel it is all command and control. It seems like the senior pastor believes he is empowering, but the staff perceives they can't make the necessary decisions to move forward.

Sometimes when I describe an empowerment culture, people say, "Oh, I thought we were an empowerment organization. However, now that you have defined it, I guess we are not." Another response I may hear is one of confusion. Since people aren't empowered with a clearly defined purpose or vision, nobody is sure what they are authorized to do. A healthy empowerment culture must include a clear vision, so those empowered will know when they are successful. Empowerment leadership is one key element that all growing churches and organizations have in common. Let's move on to the second element of the empowerment equation, which discusses what churches or organizations are empowered to accomplish.

Chapter 8 Reflection Questions

1. Before reading this chapter, how would you have answered the question: "What is the one thing needed for church growth?" Has your viewpoint changed, and in what ways?

2. Has your leadership mindset been one of command and control or empowerment? How has that manifested itself?

3. How do you view mistakes? How can mistakes be beneficial to you as an individual or in your organization?

4. If you have implemented empowerment leadership, has it been effective? In what ways?

[1] http://www.culturebydesign.co.nz/articles/command-and-control-hierarchy-to-people-centered-egalitarianism-3-tips-to-help-with-the-transformation/ accessed 11/19/2018

[2] http://edison.rutgers.edu/newsletter9.html accessed 02/24/2019

[3] https://www.inc.com/tim-donnelly/brilliant-failures/9-inventions-made-by-mistake.html accessed 08/20/2018

http://www.yurtopic.com/society/history/popular-invention-mistakes.html accessed 05/07/2019

[4] http://www.dictionary.com/browse/empowerment accessed 05/04/2019

Chapter 9: Empowered to...

Empowerment is a remarkable power-packed principle because we release people's God-given gifts and abilities for success. For this principle to be fruitful, there must be a clearly stated outcome. It's great that we understand the potential of empowerment, but as crazy as it seems, we still may not experience success when using it unless we properly direct it.

In our story of Kodak, employees could be empowered to make film all day long, and the market would still yawn and walk away, gravitating toward a digital-camera solution. As I mentioned in the earlier chapters of this book, I believe this is precisely what has happened to the Church today, thinking their main product is a church service. How many millennials do you know that are actively pondering what church service to go to? You're right! Very few. That is exactly the point; it demonstrates our disconnect with the needs of society. Currently, many in our communities see the Church as irrelevant. Young people have the viewpoint they can make a difference in the world with their buying decisions, recycling, and social justice programs. These individuals see the Church as sitting and talking but never activating. We say people matter, we say we love people, but they see us as hypocrites because stereotypically we haven't done a thing to enrich society or help our fellow man except provide a weekly church service of questionable value.

This critical view of the Church may be inaccurate because many church leaders do want to improve society; they just need to learn how to empower their congregation to do so. While empowerment is essential, it is not the entire answer to church growth. Successful empowerment requires a more detailed line of questioning starting with, "What are the people empowered to do?" We need a vision that directs people's efforts to move forward with a specific plan and purpose to meet someone's needs. What problems are people empowered to solve?

I'm Not into Lima Beans

Last night I concluded it was time to get my hair cut. I generally go to a local franchise men's hair salon, where a random person cuts my hair each time. Last night that person was a 21-year-old girl, and during the conversation, she indicated she was living with her boyfriend. Then she turned the conversation back to me, in first-rate customer service fashion by asking me what I did for a living. I replied, "I'm a pastor." Keeping the dialogue going, I asked her what she thought about church and her answer was very typical. "Church is fine as long as they don't condemn others or push it on people. We are all on our own journey and shouldn't judge other people."

It's like, "Hey I'm glad you're into your thing of making pottery but don't judge me if I'm not into it." She didn't see the value of church or what it had to offer. "Yeah, I tried it when I was younger, but it didn't appeal to me." For a minute I thought we were talking about lima beans! "Yes, my mom had me try those when I was younger, but they're not for me." I'm not putting the hairdresser down; she gave me her honest reflections to my questions. I think the bigger problem is that we have misrepresented the loving Creator of the Universe to be on par with lima beans.

Pray for Me

Let's think about it this way. Can we agree that humankind was made in the image of God (Genesis 1:27)? Good. Can we also concede that God loves all mankind (John 3:16)? I didn't say He likes what everyone does, I just said He made humanity in His image, and He loves us. I guess we could also assume that He wants us to get to know Him better and have a better life (Psalm 1:1-3, Matthew 6:33). With this in mind, there are millions of people in all sorts of less than desirable circumstances. Of these millions of people, do you think they possibly wish things were better? Of course they do! Maybe they make an inner plea to an unseen higher power for help or assistance in their situation. If you were an all-loving God, would you want to help these people that were made in your image move closer to having a relationship with you? Of course you would! So how does God help these people? We know that God knows every hair on their head and every prayer, even before they utter it (Luke 12:7, Matthew 6:8). I'm sure He wants to do something to help them.

Almost everything God does on earth, He does through people. Maybe He searches the countryside for someone gifted with abilities and willing to meet the needs of these people. It appears that God is continually looking for people to work through to accomplish His will. In 1 Corinthians 3:9-10, the Bible says we are coworkers with Him. Paul then talks about being graced or gifted by God to function as an expert builder for the Kingdom of God. This means God is looking for someone to work with Him, using the attributes He has given.

I think when the Holy Spirit hears people's inward cries or prayers for help, He is searching the earth for individuals who can help Him answer them. The Holy Spirit might be saying, "Who could help these people with their addictions? Who could help these people living on the streets? Who could visit and speak truth to men and women incarcerated, or their children who are forgotten and left behind on the outside? Who could minister to those who have not yet heard the Gospel? Is there anyone who has My heart and cares about the lost and hurting? My people have been made in My image and have been graced and given My gifts and abilities for Kingdom results. What are they doing with these abilities?" I can imagine that the Holy Spirit may grieve when He sees many people using their gifts and amazing God-given abilities for secular success because much of the worldwide Church doesn't know how to empower and help God's people for Kingdom success.

The Holy Spirit could be looking to us to be the supernatural connection where the ability of God can be released to meet a need. We are earthly God Pods designed and equipped to be guided by the Holy Spirit to be the answer to someone's prayer for help. When we follow His leading to meet their need, that is a supernatural convergence.

The Convergence Principle

Convergence simply means "the coming together of two things." In our case, hopefully, it is intersecting with the world to meet their needs and moving them toward the Kingdom of God. Convergence sounds complicated, but all you must remember is *meet people's needs*. Currently, the Church is on one trajectory, and the world is on another. The world naturally flows away from God, so we either need to make ourselves attractive with relevant answers to people's needs so the world will be drawn toward us, or we need to reach out and collide with their needs, or both.

Meet a Need

Remember years ago in your less than exciting geometry class when the teacher talked about two lines coming together and intersecting? That intersection is what we are trying to accomplish with society. We, as a church, are trying to meet and connect with people in our communities. Remember the business principle to "find a need and fill it" back in Chapter Two, the one that inspires startup companies? While people have an enormous amount of needs, if we will find just one need and fill it, this can be the basis for a successful business. Every organization exists to solve someone's demand for a product or service. The better companies address people's needs, the more successful they are. Answering needs is the *only* reason a business exists.

Does this have anything to do with the success of our churches populating the Kingdom of God? Absolutely. We can learn from businesses. The better companies meet the needs of the public, the more successful they will be. Likewise, the better we meet the needs of people, the more successful we will be about our Father's business of winning the lost for Him. All the issues people have in life add up to a massive amount of needs, and it is our job to intersect them with a solution. When we do, great things happen. We are empowered God Pods full of answers that we can supply society with, which can bring them closer to a relationship with Him. Intersecting with people to meet their needs is a convergence point where the power of God is released through us, creating a demand for more God Pods as those people bring their friends and family who also have needs to be met.

Empowered Business

The more successful a company is, the more employees they have empowered to meet market needs. There are numerous companies with over 100,000 workers worldwide to help the company succeed by meeting people's needs. How successful they are is based on these individuals working in their innate God Pod abilities and developed skill sets to solve the needs of their customers. Similarly, when we look at the most successful churches of our time, we see a high volume of volunteer teams and paid staff who are working together for Kingdom success. One of the largest churches in the world is Yoido Full Gospel Church in South Korea. It originally started in 1958 with five people, and now it reportedly has approximately 800,000 members. I'm sure there are tens of thousands of volunteers and staff to make this happen, and they must be meeting people's needs, or people wouldn't be flocking to services by the hundreds of thousands. By the way, does this sound like a church of empowerment or command and control, where the pastor needs to know every detail of what is going on? I couldn't imagine knowing all of the volunteers, let alone the 800,000 attendees! Effectively coordinating this massive amount of people is where empowerment leadership comes in.

The One Principle for Church Success

And this leads us to the answer we have been building up to over the last several chapters. Drum roll, please!

What is the one thing needed for church growth? The answer is...When we **strategically empower people to release their God-given talents and abilities in a focused direction to meet people's needs**, churches can't help but grow. If the church persistently helps new people identify their gifts and callings and use them to strategically meet a market need, the godly problem-solving engine will continue to grow. Every community has different needs. The needs of people 20 years ago may not be relevant today. We need to keep meeting the current needs of people we serve by empowering people to do it.

A Riddle

Here is a riddle: What do the most successful businesses, churches, organizations, and even countries all have in common? Answer: They all have utilized the God-Pod-gifted abilities of individuals strategically to meet a need. The entities that do this the best achieve the highest levels of success. Think of the largest and most successful companies of our time. They have harnessed human resources and technology that were specifically designed and created by gifted individuals to serve a need of mankind. As of this writing, Walmart reportedly employs 2,300,000 people. Amazon has 566,000 employees, Kroger has 449,000, Home Depot has 413,000, and the list goes on.[1] Does Walmart meet a need? Walmart reportedly has 275 million customers a week at more than 11,300 stores in 27 countries.[2] There is a very close correlation between successful organizations and how well they unleash individuals' God-given abilities toward specific outcomes. We have already noted that the same thing applies in the church world. The most successful churches have also strategically organized employees and volunteers to serve humanity.

Business Example

The following story was relayed regarding how well JetBlue does at empowering its employees to solve problems around a set of core values and create an excellent experience for its customers.

The story started a while back while I was sitting on the runway in Orlando as my homeward-bound JetBlue flight was about to taxi toward takeoff. Like just about every other flight that hadn't already been canceled that day on the Eastern seaboard, ours was a couple of hours late departing. The lead flight attendant gets on the PA system and says something very close to:

"Ladies and Gentlemen, we know we're late taking off, and even though it's the weather and not something we caused, we're going to comp everybody movies for this flight. We know you've all had a long day and we want it to end with something nice and relaxing. And for those of you who were supposed to be on the Continental flight and ended up here, we don't ever want you to go back."

The mood on the flight, which could have been a rather dreary late evening affair, took an immediate upswing. People joked and smiled and made eye contact. They were noticeably brighter and calmer as the flight progressed.

What enabled this relatively small act of kindness and allowed it to become a major brand statement? Mid-flight, I went to the back of the plane and asked. I wanted to know the policy that allowed a flight attendant to make such a call.

"We're allowed to make almost any decision," the flight attendant explained, "as long as we can justify it by one of the airline's five core values: Safety, Caring, Integrity,

Fun, and Passion. If we can tie doing something back to one of these principles, the decision is going to be supported by the company."[3]

If secular companies have figured out how to utilize the principle of empowerment to such tremendous effect, surely the Church empowered by the Holy Spirit should be able to as well!

Crucial Point

This may seem obvious, but I feel that it needs to be stated explicitly. If we are empowering people to meet needs and not ultimately loving them by leading them to Jesus, we are about building *our* business, not our Father's business. We should be loving people and helping them in their life situations; however, if we aren't sharing Jesus and changing their eternal destination, we are wasting the God Pod abilities of ourselves and our congregation. If this is the case, we are working for another kingdom instead of our Father's, and the Biblical implication is that we will be rewarded, but it is not going to be with "Well done."

Eugene Peterson in The Message translation puts it this way in his paraphrase of Matthew 7:21-23:

> "Knowing the correct password—saying 'Master, Master,' for instance—isn't going to get you anywhere with me. What is required is serious obedience—doing what my Father wills. I can see it now—at the Final Judgment thousands strutting up to me and saying, 'Master, we preached the Message, we bashed the demons, our God-sponsored projects had everyone talking.' And do you know what I am going to say? 'You missed the boat. All you did was

use me to make yourselves important. You don't impress me one bit. You're out of here.'"

Empowerment concepts are incredibly powerful; they will work to build a successful business, organization, or church. However, there should be a warning label, "Please seek the wisdom of the Bible and the Holy Spirit!" Your use of empowerment in a proper way has significant accountability attached to it. Yes, empowerment will build a church with a large attendance, but it's more than numbers. It is about our Biblical responsibility to connect people with Jesus, their Savior. If you aren't doing that, I don't want to stand next to you when Jesus is asking you about it.

Empowerment Extended

The idea of an empowered church culture does not just include the leadership team. Empowerment extends to every person and every volunteer that enters our doors. We will discuss more of the details regarding how to accomplish this in the next chapter. For now, let's take a few minutes to imagine what it would be like for each area of our church to function at its maximum empowered potential where we show special interest in every person who attends.

We talked about this vision in the God Pod Chapter but let's expand it even further. If we allow and encourage people to work in their callings and giftings, the result should be fantastic! Every area of our church would be staffed by prayed up, loving people—happily developing and utilizing their abilities for Kingdom success. The parking lot people would welcome each person with a wave and a warm smile. On rainy days, they could even hand out umbrellas so people would stay dry on their walk to the entry doors. Greeters would look forward to loving and caring for each person that came in, possibly sensing whether attendees needed prayer or personal assistance. The praise and worship team would earnestly pray and practice the preceding week to usher people into the very presence of God. From the pulpit, there would be excellent and engaging teaching that not only provoked people to acts of love and kindness but also drew them closer to a meaningful relationship with God.

This culture of prayer, love, and empowerment would saturate our staff, volunteer teams, and ultimately our entire congregations. The results of empowerment would be that we would have phenomenal praise and worship, an incredibly engaging children's ministry, and a world-class youth ministry. Every area of our church would be striving to be the best it could be to achieve eternal Kingdom results. Yes, our congregation would be better; but the outcome would be much more extensive than just producing a more effective church service. Our whole community would be enriched and encouraged not only through our congregation but also through thriving outreach ministries, influencing every area of our city.

Our community ministries would help with practical needs—everything from divorce and grief recovery to achieving financial stability. The ministry outreach options are almost endless. All these areas would be operated by gifted people from our congregation, using their abilities in specific areas of ministry. All these activities would take place because there is a culture of empowerment, and we empower people in our congregation to succeed to their "Well done." To do this, we would have a process that helps these individuals identify their gifts and abilities, and then move forward to a life of fulfillment and joy. We would have an entire congregation of people who are walking in peace and contentment but also striving forward, knowing they were precisely where God called them to be.

Because our congregation is a safe, accepting, and loving environment people would be free to share and shed their burdens. The result of people walking in true godly freedom, confident in their place in the Body of Christ and using their gifts and talents for Kingdom growth, would result in better marriages, better workplaces, thriving children and family relationships, and on and on. Every area of life would be better; it would be saturated with God's goodness and grace. The natural outcome of this type of environment is a congregation of loving people who, in turn, would love to serve others. Their devotion would extend to every area people are involved in, from the homeless, to those in jails and prisons, and from senior citizens in nursing homes, to the boardrooms of our city. Everyone would be affected and influenced positively with the very essence of an all-loving Father flowing through the people of His Church. Isn't this the church you want to attend? I sure do. It is a church where people are released and empowered to be representatives of Christ to those around them.

Empowerment Value

If our goal is to produce this God-saturated, empowered atmosphere the results would be amazing. There is no way people would ever want to leave your church with this type of environment. Wouldn't it be a great goal to give people so much God value through your church that there is no way they would ever consider going anywhere else? Isn't that the example our Father gave us? Jesus, the ultimate servant-leader, has given us so much value, why would we go anywhere except to Him? With Jesus, our sins are forgiven, we have eternal life, and He gave us the Holy Spirit, our counselor, peace, and teacher. Jesus has served us by giving His very life, and I don't want to go anywhere else; nowhere else remotely compares to His presence. The empowerment process would repeat itself as new people attend church. They would get healthy, grow, and after discovering their talents and abilities, also gladly take their place in the Body of Christ serving others. The results seem a little like Heaven, but isn't that what Jesus prayed? "Your Kingdom come, Your will be done on earth as it is in Heaven."

Now it is up to us to create this same environment for people who are impacted by our churches, and then maybe the very essence of Jesus' prayer can take place in our communities.

Empowered Status Quo

Before we can make this transformation in our churches and communities, it is vital to have a concrete understanding of how the concept of convergence impacts the implementation of empowerment leadership. It is not enough to empower people. We need to release and enable them in a specific direction to solve people's needs. I have heard too many pastors say, "Mac, we are empowering our people." I say, "Cool, what are they empowered to do?" Often, I find out they are not empowered to solve real needs of the community, but rather the needs of the church. They are empowered to continue to do church the same way it has been. Once again, I'm not against having church services. We need people who function to maintain and facilitate the church and its services, but what is the end game? Are we going through the motions of having church services for ourselves and other Christians, or are we about our Father's business with innovative ways to transform lives in our communities for the Kingdom?

Church Equals Facilitators

What if we, as church leaders, were focused on serving two groups of people? First, we accepted the responsibility as Maxwell says, "Everything rises and falls on leadership." Next, we became servant-leaders or facilitators to serve our congregations to hear, "Well done," by helping them discover the gifts of God on their life. To do this, we need a process that allows them to identify their gifts and then be empowered to use those to serve the second group of people, those outside the walls of the church. What if we became co-laborers with Christ for Biblical convergence where we intersected with hurting people and became the release point of God's goodness and love to influence others? In short, what if we became the long-awaited answer to others' prayers?

What if the Church was not known for being a service or a building, but facilitators and empowerers that released and directed the gifts of God to help other people? What if we were known for activating people to serve, and changing lives throughout our community? What if we became an incubator designed at facilitating people toward Kingdom success with teams or entry points where people could progress, grow, and be discipled to godly success?

Maybe if we did these things, church leadership would hear our Father say, "Well done!"

This active approach to making a godly impact in our churches and communities is reflected within the powerful words of the Matthew West song, "Do Something." In the song he asks God to take action in response to all the troubles in the world with the question, "God, why don't you do something?" God's poignant answer is, "I did. I created you."[4]

Convergence: The Intersection of God's Goodness

God has a plan not only to change our lives but to use us to change others' lives as well. What a privilege, that once we get saved, we have talents we can use for Kingdom purposes. If someone excels in music, now they can use that skill for the Kingdom of God. If someone has an administrative gift or is graced with the gift of hospitality, mercy, or any other ability, we can use these things for Kingdom purposes. God has gifted each person with a skill or talent that can be used for Him.

The principle of convergence occurs when our abilities and gifts collide with someone else's needs in a God-ordained supernatural connection. Our job as church leaders is to acknowledge and direct this powerful principle for Kingdom growth. Every day people are consciously or unconsciously praying for answers in their life. People have a multitude of problems, and they are inwardly crying out for answers. People are looking for answers to confusion, depression, heartache, addictions, loss, etc. On the flip side, there are people who are called and gifted by God to meet these and other needs. Men and woman of God will not be content unless they fulfill the God-ordained path for their life. This is the opportunity for a supernatural convergence of a life changed for the Kingdom. Many lives will not be changed unless you and I, who are gifted with answers, do our part to deliver His solution. As leaders in our local churches, we can either hinder these connections or actively facilitate and encourage them.

Ultimately, I don't care if we position ourselves so that we run into the world, or we position ourselves so the world is drawn to us. The main thing is that we create a point of connection. Generally, since the world is not going to flow toward the Church, it is up to us to see how we can relate to the world. We can connect with them by helping them solve their needs. Once we intersect with individuals of the world, we can guide them along. Think of a river joining up with a smaller stream. The stream becomes absorbed and part of the larger, stronger path of water. The river indicates the direction and ultimate destination of the smaller influenced body of water. Wouldn't it be great to absorb a multitude of people trapped in the sin of the world, successfully arriving at the ultimate final destination of Heaven and hearing, "Well done," together?

Start Here

The ways to intersect with the world are almost endless. I like to start with what needs I can fulfill and see how I can use this solution to influence others. If there is a big homeless problem and I don't feel that is where I'm gifted, I may not have the passion or understanding of how to effectively solve it. I want to start with the gifts of God and calling on my life and then pray about how I can meet others' needs with that. Say I'm a musician and I feel called to serve the homeless. Maybe I can team up with someone who can prepare food, and we create a ministry around food and music. Perhaps every week, we set up in an appropriate area to distribute food and play music. This can open recurrent ministry opportunities. As you pray, seek God's wisdom and direction; He usually gives clues on how to proceed. Think of Moses when he led the people out of Egypt. God asked him, "What is in your hand?" It was a rod, and God used it to ultimately free the people (Exodus 4:2). I'm confident no matter what Moses would have answered, God would have said, "No problem, that will work." You can cut hair? That will work. You can sew? Excellent. You can fix cars?

That works. Writing? I can use that. Social media? Sounds good. Change a baby's diaper? Perfect. If we dedicate our gift to God, whatever it may be, He can touch lives with it. So, what is in your hand?

One church that I know of had an out-of-the-box plan to intersect with the world. The senior pastor had some contacts in the world of professional rodeo, and God put it on his heart to start a rodeo camp for teens. This wasn't a rinky-dink operation with some local cowboys who went to a few junior rodeos when they were kids. God gave him tremendous favor, and the instructors at the camp were world champions in their areas. Kids came from all over the region, even out of state, to attend the camp. They spent their days learning high-level skills from champion athletes who cared about them. They were also cared for and encouraged by others in the church who worked selflessly, making meals and helping with all the details of the camp. The evenings were spent at worship services with the champion athletes, who shared their life-changing testimonies of connecting with Jesus. Not only did attendees receive the best possible instruction in their competitive discipline, but they were also given the good news of the Gospel from men and women who were true role models, as they loved God and excelled as professional athletes. The camp ran for years and impacted hundreds of families. Again I ask, what is in your hand?

Two Needs

The Holy Spirit once told me, "Mac, people come to a church for the same reasons they come to a business. Number one, I have a problem or need, and I hope this place can help me. Number two, I have talents that can be helpful to others, and maybe this place can utilize those abilities."

The same two main reasons people go to a business are the same two reasons people come to our churches each week. Unfortunately, we usually don't think about why people inconvenience themselves to show up to our church, we are just glad they did, and we want them to stay. While we have spent a fair amount of time looking at how we can meet the needs of those who come to us with problems to solve, we cannot ignore the second reason people come to our churches.

"I'm Done with This Church"

There is a growing segment of society that has been labeled "The Dones." These are people who were very involved in their church but became disillusioned for a variety of reasons and left. There are three very notable attributes about The Dones. First of all, they were highly active in their churches. These were not freeloaders or consumers of the Church. They were committed participants, generally well-integrated into the leadership structure of the Church. Secondly, they didn't want to leave. The church filled several their spiritual and social needs. Walking away from those connections was not an easy decision. Finally, The Dones felt stifled by the church structure. Many of them still want to serve mankind, and so they join organizations not associated with Christianity that allow them to continue to serve and impact their communities.[5] This should be a gigantic lesson for us. The Dones are people who love God, were active and devoted to their church, and now they feel it is less complicated and more beneficial for them to serve outside a Christian structure. Ouch! What a colossal pushback against our current non-empowerment church structure. Why would people who love God and enjoyed the church they were serving in, feel like it was in their best interest to leave the place they cared about and were fulfilling the call of God on their lives, to serve their fellow man through a secular organization? The Dones are fed up with the current bureaucracy of the Church, and they feel they are better off staying away from it, yet they still enjoy serving. Unfortunately, this is a less than positive reflection on the Church today.

If we are doing things correctly, the opposite should be taking place at church. People will be waiting in line and bringing their friends with them. Isn't this what happens when a great store, restaurant, or a blockbuster movie opens? People change their plans, call in sick to work, and go pick up their friends just to attend a movie about a fictitious superhero. We have the real superhero, King Jesus, who literally gave His life to save all of humanity!

Some people get so caught up in thinking this is how we have always done church, while the world is going to Hell because we are determined not to change. No offense, but chances are things have changed a bit since Peter, John, and the bros were walking around in their nightgowns and flip flops behind Jesus. Change doesn't mean embracing society's values, but it's hard to love people into the Kingdom when they feel like we don't like them or can't relate to them. Jesus showed us how He could love people and accept them unconditionally without condoning their lifestyle. This is a beautiful example of convergence. Jesus was always considering how He could intersect and interact with people who needed Him. We don't need to like or embrace what the world does, but we do need to understand where they are, care about them, and relate to them. Or we could keep doing the same thing with the same results, and not fulfill the Great Commission. Now that would be a bummer.

The Unified Body of Christ

Now let's take things a crazy step further. Before Jesus left, He instructed His believers to walk in unity (John 17:21). Can this be established in an empowerment culture that is working toward convergence, serving its community? Let's take a look. One of the critical elements of empowerment is building teams of people who are working together for the same outcome. With this structure, we don't need individual control or care who gets the credit because our focus is on the result. In an empowerment culture, it is about everyone taking their place, functioning for a Kingdom win for the Body of Christ. What this means is that we will see churches that are naturally more gifted in different serving capacities because of the abilities in individual people and the mandate they have from God. Some churches will be better at jail and prison ministry based on God's giftings and favor. Since success isn't predicated on getting the credit, but rather the outcomes, these churches are looking to network and connect with other churches and organizations for maximum effectiveness. I think God designed it so we will never experience maximum success without unifying as the Body of Christ. Churches and groups may be thinking, "Hey, you have connections I don't have, and I have resources you don't have. If we teamed up, we could do great things for the Kingdom." This is the right attitude and the behaviors we were instructed to pursue. Would this change society's view of us if we, as individual churches within the Body of Christ, not only refused to talk negatively about each other, but went on to love, pray for, and unite together for a strategic Kingdom outcome?

Convergence What If

What if, as the Body of Christ, His Church, we became great at helping people discover the gifts and abilities on their lives and then we had a system to help them activate those talents based on the God-given passions of the Holy Spirit on the inside of them? What if we really understood our communities' needs, and we became the God-empowered convergent solution where those gifts of God could be released strategically to change lives? What if we looked to unite with other churches in the Body of Christ to leverage our effectiveness and success? The result could be pastors, leaders, and congregations that hear, "Well done, thou good and faithful servant."

I know what you could be thinking if you are not the senior pastor leading your church. "Mac, this all sounds great, but I'm...well, what can I do?" Fill in the blank with your mental response. Let's answer that fundamental question next!

Chapter 9 Reflection Questions

1. How well is your church doing at meeting community needs? What is working?

2. What are the steps that you could take to empower people in your organization toward a common goal/purpose? Articulate the common purpose.

3. What are some ways that you can position yourself/your organization to run into the world, or draw the world toward you?

4. How can you engage "The Dones" in your community?

5. What are some ways that you could foster cooperation and unity with other churches and organizations in your community?

[1] https://en.wikipedia.org/wiki/List_of_largest_employers_in_the_United_States accessed 05/07/2019

[2] https://corporate.walmart.com/our-story accessed 02/28/2019

[3] https://digitalsparkmarketing.com/employee-empowerment/ accessed 02/28/2019

[4] https://www.bing.com/search?FORM=U162DF&PC=U162&q=matthew+west+do+something+lyrics accessed 05/07/2019

[5] https://www.christianitytoday.com/pastors/2015/summer-2015/meet-dones.html accessed 11/20/2018

Chapter 10: I'm Not the Pastor or Leader So...

What Can I Do?

A valid question I often hear goes like this, "Mac, your ideas seem right, and I believe they will work, but I'm not the senior pastor or leader of the company. I don't have any decision-making authority at the church or organization, so what can I do?" While I think it's a great question, we can ask it two different ways. The first option is to come wringing our hands whimpering, "I'm a poor pathetic victim, woe is me. There is nothing I can do." Or we can ask, "What can I change about my actions to make a positive impact?" It is so easy to point at someone else as the problem and be unwilling to change ourselves. Spouses do this all the time. Oops! Did I type that? The problem with that mindset is that we are the only people we can ultimately change. If we work on ourselves first, it is possible we can ultimately influence others to change. However, it all starts with us.

Continual Prayer

I want to give tangible answers but understand the first and ongoing action must be prayer. Pray, pray, and then pray some more. Pray for your pastor and leadership. Pray for your leaders to have a heart to hear from God.

Pray for wisdom and direction for what God would have you do to move forward. Believe God will listen to and answer your prayers. God said, "If My people who are called by My name will humble themselves, and pray and seek My face, and turn from their wicked ways, then I will hear from heaven, and will forgive their sin and heal their land. (2 Chron 7:14 NIV) Pray and do what He says to do.

Leadership Is Influence

Let's take a step back and look to the writings of John Maxwell again. In his book, *The 21 Irrefutable Laws of Leadership,* he states that "The true measurement of leadership is influence—nothing more, nothing less." Can you influence an organization when you are not at the top? Sure, because if influence is leadership, influence isn't dependent on being at the top. In fact, Maxwell wrote an entire book on this concept and coined the term "360-Degree Leader." The basic premise is that you can lead from anywhere in the organization—up, down, and across. The best way to apply influential leadership "up" is to serve your leaders and help them accomplish their goals. We should be helping leadership solve their problems. Normally a leader doesn't say, "I don't want you to help me accomplish my goals." When I come alongside leaders and serve them with the agenda to help them meet their needs and improve and accomplish their mission, things seem to work out. To lead "across," we apply some of the same principles and help those alongside us win as well. In this manner, we are leaders of other leaders—helping our peers to accomplish their goals. Rather than competing with them, we work to complete projects and initiatives with them. Now I'm not saying there won't be any bumps or misunderstandings along the way. Others have misread my actions and motives countless times, but my goal to keep serving remains the same.

When we lead "down," we help those below us realize their potential and encourage them to become a part of a larger purpose...God Pods, anyone?!?

Influential Leadership Examples

Let me give you some examples of 360-Degree Leadership. At our church, we have a first-rate facilities and custodial team. They are fantastic and have happy, joyous attitudes while serving and doing what most would call menial jobs. I can assure you that their great demeanor and hearts to serve are contagious; they are 360-Degree Leaders and they positively influence the people around them. Others can't help but be affected by them because they are so hard working and have such an exceptional serving attitude. This team is almost legendary; they have gladly worked all night to complete construction or cleaning projects, all without being asked because it is just their heart to serve. Our usher's team is the same way. The ushers man the doors and walk through the halls, smiling and searching for people to help, speaking an encouraging word, or removing a shred of paper off the floor. After a service one cold winter evening, the ushers lined up at the main exit to thoughtfully walk each woman that needed assistance safely across an icy parking lot to their car. They continually seek to serve and bless all those around them. Here is the truth: We are all influencers. We all influence people, whether for good or bad, in everything we do. The key is, how are we influencing and ultimately leading them? Are the people around us being encouraged and blessed, or do they feel like they are working with Eeyore from The Hundred Acre Wood? Do we bring a heaviness into the room when we enter it, or are we an upbeat, encouraging example of loving and serving others?

Not being the senior pastor means I don't know every detail or all the specifics of what the pastor is trying to accomplish. That is not important. If I know the big concept of what they want to do, I can be a positive instrument of change in the overall organization. I'm going to make some general assumptions: Does the senior pastor want a healthy organization of people with a great attitude? Yes. Do they want the church to grow? Yes. Think of how many things I can do to be a positive influence in just these areas. I can continually read and study on the topic of positive growth and talk about it all the time. I can set the example of inviting and greeting new people. I can relay positive testimonies of lives changed and the church influence increasing. I can spend time in the Bible, so I have an encouraging word from God to speak to those I encounter. There are endless positive things I can do from any position in our church structure, from a volunteer up, that can have a gigantic effect on others to help create a thriving, positive environment. There are many things I can do to create positive growth that the senior pastor cannot in his/her role. From my serving position, I can lend positive energy, and support what the pastor wants to accomplish, influencing those in my sphere more effectively because I have already built a rapport with them. It is up to me to be the best I can, and yes, to serve my pastor. Ultimately, I'm working for My Father in Heaven, a valuable perspective we all need to maintain.

Leadership Starts with Me

If I want to be a godly, influential leader, then I must realize that leadership must start with me first. I must lead myself positively, or no one else should follow me. I need to be the example I want other people to be. When I attend church, am I on time? Am I attentive, smiling, and listening to the pastor? Do I bring my Bible? Do I take notes? Am I interested in and learning from the sermon? Am I a participant or just a spectator? We have all seen the people half asleep in church or playing on their phones. Really, why did they come? Yes, the pastor has a responsibility to seek God for the sermon and direction for the congregation, but it is up to us to attentively hear the message that the Holy Spirit is trying to get to us. Once again, it is our responsibility to be an example of how others should be. If we were the senior pastor, would we like the entire congregation filled with people just like us, dedicated like we are? Who tithe as we do? Who serve as we do? Who worship as we do? Who pray for the pastor and leadership as we do? Being the example of the people we would like the Church to be full of is an excellent foundational step to influential leadership that has a vision for church growth.

Double or Half

In teaching me about leadership, my mentors relayed a concept about how often people will follow leaders' examples. They told me, "Unfortunately, people will copy about half of your positive behaviors, and they will double your negative ones." So, if you speak poorly about the pastor, the people you influence will talk twice as badly. If you show up late to church services, your team will. If you attend every service, your team will show up about half of the time. If you are reading your Bible and praying for your pastor, your followers will adhere to your example to some extent.

In my experience, the concept is generally very true; observe those around you. I think you will notice the same thing. Those influenced by us do about half of the positive things we do, but they multiply the negative things we do. While we can pretend to have the admirable traits we want to have and see in others, if we are faking it, the truth will radiate through. We need to truly be transformed and become the people God wants us to be. We are all influencers/leaders; it is up to us to be the genuine, godly example of how we want others to be as directed by Jesus' standards.

360-Degree Movie

The 2015 film *The Intern*, with Robert De Niro and Anne Hathaway, does a great job reflecting the concept of a 360-Degree Leader. If you haven't already seen it, I encourage you to do so. It is an outstanding story in which the intern is initially disregarded but winds up to be the influencer and...Oh never mind, I don't want to be "that guy" that ruins the end of the movie. If you're struggling to grasp the concept of a 360-Degree Leader, this feel-good movie may clarify the role and behaviors of this type of leadership for you.

The Tipping Point

From the "lowly" intern to the greeter at the front door, or even an elder in church, everyone can create positive change within their workplace or church. There is a concept I like to teach called, "A tipping point." The tipping point has been described as "the critical point in an evolving situation that leads to a new and irreversible development...In some usage, a tipping point is simply an addition or increment that in itself might not seem extraordinary but that unexpectedly is just the amount of additional change that will lead to a big effect."[1]

Malcolm Gladwell, Canadian journalist, author, and public speaker describes this phenomenon in his book,

The Tipping Point: How Little Things Can Make a Big Difference where he defines a tipping point as "the moment of critical mass, the threshold, the boiling point." As Gladwell states, "Ideas and products and messages and behaviors spread like viruses do."[2] In essence, the concept is that we can gradually enact positive attitudes and behavioral changes that will permeate and ultimately affect the entire trajectory of our church, organization, or business.

Creating this change, we start with ourselves. We understand our influence as a leader and become the example we want the whole church or organization to follow. If we begin as the only one with a positive attitude for growth, this positivity along with behavioral change should motivate others around us—gradually creating the tipping point for positive impact throughout the entire organization. All you must do is decide your area of service or volunteerism is going to be the best area in the church. It doesn't matter whether you work on the cleaning team or as a greeter. You become an influencer, reflecting the very best you can be. Your superb approach will gradually become contagious, and soon others on your team or other teams will be catching your great attitude and serving characteristics. If you continue to encourage people and resource them with applicable materials to move forward, your influence will continue to grow, affecting more people with the empowerment vision of serving. If you stay steadfast, praying for God's wisdom and favor for your area, the tide will gradually change, and there will ultimately be a momentum shift of people moving in a new and improved direction of success. Pretty soon, because you have set the example by projecting a positive influence, there's a church full of God-honoring, positive growth-oriented people, serving the Lord and seeking to hear, "Well done." This all happened because you understood your role as an influencer and a 360-Degree Leader.

Start Here

Leaders, do you want to know how to change the culture of your church to become one of empowerment? The answer is the tipping point. If we continue to promote people's stewardship of the gifts of God within them, creating an environment where they are encouraged to find and fulfill the call of God on their life, this shifts their thoughts in a new direction, collectively. If we continually serve our people and reinforce these concepts through testimonies, recognition, and celebration, it gradually becomes their desire to achieve for the Kingdom of God. The commitment on our part must be one of relentless serving, being determined to be the example for our church or organization. When we are steadfastly committed to moving our culture to a healthy, empowered position of serving others, it will cause a tipping point which will release the God Pod abilities of people into an excited team of empowered servers for Christ.

Negative Tipping

We should be aware that tipping points can be used positively or negatively to create changes within our church, community, or even our nation. From my vantage point, society has moved in a more immoral direction over the last several decades; but how did it happen? It seems to me like the media has continually portrayed stories of sinful, sexual lifestyles as natural—glamorizing TV shows about unwed teenage mothers and entire websites, magazines, and television shows dedicated to keeping up with who is cheating on who. The media has reinforced these viewpoints with testimonies, even if they are false, isolated, or misleading. After years of this narrative, people have become desensitized to immorality. Whatever we promote, we get more of that. Our churches need to encourage positive, life-changing testimonies and continually model godly success that people will want to experience. And it all starts with positive influence from a leader like you.

Influencers Tip

Here is a tip on tipping points. My close friends and business associates often won't listen to me because I'm "just Mac." I'm nothing special. I'm the guy they have known and worked with for years; I can't be or know anything extraordinary. "Nothing is amazing about Mac; we have known him forever, so why would we listen to him about making positive changes in our life?" You may have experienced something similar in how your friends see you. This can be very discouraging if we are trying to move these friends in a positive direction. So how do I enact change with naysayers around me? What do I do to influence them?

First, it's up to me to be a positive example by continually maintaining a great attitude. Next, we should acknowledge and encourage others when we see them make movements in a positive direction. It can be as simple as, "John, I've noticed you're getting bolder in befriending new people. Great job!" The next key is to offer or suggest audio or visual resources that contain the messages we want to convey to the people we want to help change. I've found great resources that have changed my life and know that others would also benefit from them. So, I pass along this helpful information by encouraging them to watch or listen to those resources. I try not to tell them what to do. Instead, I say, "I listened to an excellent audio by this lady; it has amazing information. I think you would like it. Would you be open to listening to it?" Resources might include books, audiobooks, podcasts, blogs, articles, or other helpful information that will help, influence, and grow yourself and others. For instance, I wrote this book as a resource you can use to help influence people in your church or organization for positive change. If you like these ideas and you think they would help your church or organization, use it as a tool to help influence them.

Utilizing resources is a massive key to changing a culture. I have given away hundreds of books and audios over the years. I have bought cases of books to distribute. Why? Because the author spent years writing out what I wish I could say, and I used their work as a cultural change resource. A book is a very cheap investment to change your culture. Don't get discouraged; some people won't want to grow now, but keep serving and resourcing the ones that want to by planting the seeds of positive change. And don't forget to keep praying! It's like the parable of the sower. Your job is to keep planting if you want a Kingdom harvest.

Haven't you seen this principle work with your kids? You can tell your kids 300 times that they should work hard in school, but it falls on deaf ears. When you talk with them, they react like a petrified zombie and stare into space. However, if someone they look up to casually mentions the importance of school to your children, it appears the wisdom came straight from a burning bush, or the heavens opened, and there was a booming voice saying, "Hey, you should apply yourself in school!" They immediately make a 180-degree change and become the best students in school. They look at you and say, "Why didn't you ever tell me how important school is and that I should work hard?" Their whole life changes because an outsider was used as a resource, shared some insights and changed their life. I'm not upset. I'm just rejoicing that the kids are now moving in a positive direction. As influencers, it is smart to use the resources of successful people to guide our culture in a new direction that will benefit them.

Microwave Popcorn

Influencing a church or organization to a tipping point is like cooking microwave popcorn. What is it with me and popcorn analogies? Anyway, you put the popcorn bag in the microwave, hit the start button, and voila! Nothing happens. However if you keep the power on (stay consistent with your positive attitude and influence), gradually a few kernels take the initiative to follow your leadership example and...POP! If you continue to stay consistent with the power on, soon there is a tipping point, and then there's a gigantic flurry of popping seeds.

This creates a chain reaction, and nearly all at once, the culture of the bag changes. The kernels are empowered to become all that God intended them to be, puffy, savory, and buttery popcorn. Delicious! Do all the seeds pop? I don't think I have ever had all the kernels pop in any microwave popcorn bag. I can focus all my efforts on these unpoppable ones, and I will never have a tasty bag of popcorn to eat. Instead, I need to work with the people who are ready and want to move forward, and their momentum will help others pop into success, many of whom might not otherwise have done so on their own. And whatever you do, don't stop and start the process. The power of your prayers and great attitude must remain on to keep that momentum going, resulting in an enlarged congregation full of people "popping" into the men and women of God that they were called to be and influencing others for Christ.

Steps to Create a Tipping Point

1. Be the example: Pray, behave, act, and talk the way you want others to.

2. Use resources: Freely give out resources that support positive change.

3. Publicly celebrate the positive behaviors people exhibit toward the new culture.

4. Publicly proclaim testimonies from people impacted by the change.

5. Continually share the vision of a changed organization.

6. Support others championing positive change.

7. Do not grow weary in well-doing.

8. Repeat.

Paradigm Shift

Once again, in the tipping equation, we are the key. We are the example—praying, hard work, positive attitude, continual learning, etc. We always start with us; then we influence our team through our example and resources. We change. Our area changes. Then other areas are affected to change and grow, which will positively impact our whole church or organization. But what if we shared what was working for our church with other churches? What if we remembered that we were all followers of

Christ and on the same team as the Body of Christ? What if we recognized we are all serving the same Father, and we will all be in Heaven together for eternity? What if we prayed blessings on and walked in unity with other churches because that is what Jesus told us to do—to be unified?

My viewpoint is if I can figure out how to help the Body of Christ grow, I need to share it with others because we are ultimately all working on the same team for one Leader. If the church right across the street from ours needs help to grow, I want to help them. I'm going to share with them all I can in hopes that their church will explode with new growth. I want them and all the Jesus-promoting churches in our community to expand exponentially, and then start other dynamic growing churches, ultimately serving our community to Christ. Isn't this the unified mindset Jesus directed us to have? Here's the thing. I have heard about a possible "last days revival," and I'm excited about it. However, there is a problem. Practically speaking, if there is a revival, all the people in our community won't fit in our church. They won't even fit in all the existing churches currently in our community. There are not enough churches in existence to put all the people I'm hoping would get saved and need a church during this time. It is my viewpoint to start a bunch of new churches and get as many existing churches healthy and thriving as possible, so when the end time revival hits, we will have a multiplicity of nets (churches) ready to bring in a bountiful harvest for the Kingdom! Ya, baby! That's what I'm talking about!

You may be saying, "Yes, Mac, but what if there isn't an end time revival?" My goal is to serve so many people and churches, resulting in so much growth and Kingdom success, that there will be a supernatural tipping point where a revival will be inevitable. And if there isn't a revival, let's go ahead and fill all the churches anyway; I'm sure Jesus won't mind.

Faster or Farther

There is a saying, "If you want to go fast, go alone. If you want to go far, go together." In our case, I'm hoping we want to go far, which means we, as the Body of Christ, need to unify and work together to make an enormous impact for a long time. Our race is not a sprint; in fact, organizations with explosive growth sometimes concern me. I like a robust and steady expansion. If organizations grow too fast, I'm concerned they may not have the systems in place necessary to sustain the increase. Think of a plant that grows rapidly without the essential root structure to maintain it or support it during turbulent times. Now think of a mighty oak with an extended root structure that can weather almost any storm. For us to be effective at impacting the world for Christ, we need to unite first as teams of people, then as a church, then, hopefully, churches can join and work together as the Body of Christ, encouraging each other to stay grounded in our faith in Jesus. With this robust root system as the unified Body of Christ, we can remain constant, grow larger, and go farther to impact the world for the Kingdom.

Tip Your Community

I would like to see churches develop and have so much impact serving and improving their communities, giving them so much value, that the residents couldn't imagine life without the presence of your church. Wouldn't it be great if lives were so affected in your community that even unbelievers spoke well of your church? You might hear, "Hey, I don't attend that church, in fact, I don't believe in God, but I know the people at that church love people. They are always reaching out to serve people who are hurting in our community." If that was the attitude, what is the possibility that if something happened in that individual's life, the Holy Spirit might use it as a way for you to connect with him, use your ability to meet his needs, and ultimately influence him for the Kingdom? Let's determine to give so much value to our communities through meeting needs that no one would want to see your church close.

Just Came In

Long after I had written the previous section the following review was posted about our church. I'm including it as an example.

"I've never attended Life Church but my experience with people from it has been amazing. I'm currently homeless here in Boise, Idaho. Today at the XXXXX Day Shelter, folks from this church stopped by to bring some well-appreciated breakfast burritos, juice, salsa, prayer cloths, Bibles, and most importantly compassion.

If folks can come down there on a cold February Saturday, show compassion for others that are in temporary bad/challenging places in life, then that shows true compassion and empathy from members of this church.

I spoke with an incredible lady named XXXX (hope I spelled her name correctly). Just so grateful. Can't wait to attend services at this church. Thank you folks. God bless you all!"

I believe that if we are serving our community correctly and giving them exceptional value, the blessings of God will be on the city and the results will be a lower crime rate, lower divorce rate, lower addiction rate, lower suicide rate, and on and on. I believe people will be able to tangibly feel and see the difference in our community. Why? Because your church is relevant; it's full of people who love serving Jesus, and you have a process to empower those people to meet needs and change lives.

Now that we understand the power of unifying and empowering people to serve others, let's discuss the practical side of how to move this forward with the steps of empowerment.

Chapter 10 Reflection Questions

1. How can you practice 360-Degree Leadership in your current position? How are you going to lead up, down, and across?

2. What steps are you going to take to lead yourself well? What kind of example are you setting by your conduct?

3. How can you use the concept of the tipping point to your advantage in creating change?

4. How can you work at building connections with other churches to walk in unity with them?

[1] https://whatis.techtarget.com/definition/tipping-point accessed 11/20/2018

[2] https://en.wikipedia.org/wiki/The_Tipping_Point accessed 11/20/2018

Chapter 11: Developing an Empowered Organization

Empowerment Unpacked

We have talked about empowerment leadership; the empowering of people to use the abilities of God or the grace of God flowing through them to meet people's needs, as the number-one key for church and organizational success. Combining this with the principles of empowerment, the topic of this chapter will create a healthy, highly effective church culture that is reaching the lost with the love of God. There is a fundamental challenge in developing this chapter. In life, many things are either art or science. Science has verifiable facts and patterns like, the average adult human body has 206 bones or "For every action, there is an equal and opposite reaction," (Newton's Third Law of Motion). These things aren't up for debate. However, art is different. I have a friend who is a brilliant artist. He can paint a landscape picture with tree trunks that are green, brown, orange, pink, or purple. He could even paint tie-dye tree trunks, and they would look great! He's a master painter and can make crazy things work together to create a fabulous painting. The reason I tell you this is that there are standard principles that work when building organizations, but there are also gifted people who can color outside the lines and still create a healthy, empowerment culture. Similar to creating a work of art, when building a successful, empowered organization there is a substantial amount of personalization and improvisation, based on the various people we are working with (our array of art supplies) and our desired outcome.

I don't have the gift of art at all, but thankfully I have the gift of organization building. If you put me with a group of people for any amount of time, soon I'm determining those individuals' strengths and abilities and how they can fit together to create an effective team. I don't need to try to see these abilities within people; it just happens because of the gifting of God on my life. This is not something I can take credit for; it is just how I'm wired by God to think. It is a challenge to write this chapter because how do I make something subjective and innate clear? In this section, I will do my best to relay those thoughts and processes.

I should also point out that there are two distinct topics that we will cover in this chapter regarding creating an empowered church, but they are deeply intertwined. The first one is how we recruit and develop the volunteer force that carries out the day-to-day ministry of the Church, and the second topic deals specifically with our paid staff: administrative, department heads, pastors, etc.

Can Anyone Build an Empowerment Organization?

Anyone can build an empowered organization, but it may require substantial changes because an empowerment culture is so different from the command and control leadership that typifies most churches and organizations (or that is stereotyped as the standard business model within TV shows and movies). There is a different set of viewpoints for empowerment organizations, but once you and your church experience the culture shift, none of you will ever want to go back. An empowerment culture unfetters the people in an organization to do what they are called and gifted to do, and it frees leadership from the burden of making every decision. With empowerment, the whole group is a vested team looking for the best solutions to move forward and accomplish goals.

Key Player

Just like any ability, building an empowerment organization is easier for some people than others. Can you do it? Yes, but the level of your success may be determined by the gifts of God on your life. Can I sing? Yes, well, sort of, depending on how loosely you define the word "sing." But my so-called singing is nothing anyone else wants to hear. Truthfully, I don't even want to listen to myself sing. So can you build an organization? Sure, but your success will be directly proportional to how much God has gifted you in this area. If you are not gifted in administration and organization building, one of the first steps you should consider is to keep your eyes open to recruit a person to help in this area. This gifted organization builder could be the most crucial recruiting decision you make in this entire process. Start where you are, putting your team together to the best of your abilities, and continually pray and look for the person with the skill set to help you build a healthy organization. A GIGANTIC warning when hiring a person to help build your organization is that they must be building the leader's vision and not their own. There are many horror stories of empowering someone to build an organization, but they lacked the leader's vision of what was to be accomplished. It is up to the leader to share the vision and continue to monitor the organization building progress, ensuring that things are moving in the right direction.

For those of you musically inclined, think of this process like building an orchestra: identifying people's aptitudes, matching each person based on their strengths with the instrument that best suits them, and then determine how the group can blend to create beautiful music. Even though the skill set of assembling an orchestra is similar to that required for building a team, you also must have a musical skill set. Likewise, you need to have a knowledge of administration and organizational building, or recruit someone who does, to make this process work effectively.

Of course, the only way to make the growth process genuinely successful is to make sure that Jesus is the Living Stone or the foundation upon which we build our lives and our house, the Church (1 Peter 2:4-5). Most of us have never constructed a building, but we have put together a puzzle.

Motto: Start with what you know and move toward it

Forming a highly effective, functioning body of believers, empowered to do the work of God, is a lot like building a puzzle. If I'm assembling a puzzle, the first thing I want to look at is the picture on the front of the box. In some cases, the Father tells us what the final structure of the organization or church we are building will look like, but in most cases, He does not. Church bodies, like people, come in all shapes and sizes, and I believe that there is an individual mandate on each of them. Some churches are geared toward training up missionaries and carrying God's Word to foreign lands. Others might be called to start a school and provide godly education to the youth of a community. Still, others might have a particular call to the elderly and offer multiple services to shut-ins and widows. Whatever the case may be, we have at least some Biblical indications regarding what a fruitful church should look like, so we should start building toward what we know and get additional tips from the Holy Spirit as we proceed. This is the first of our principles for empowerment.

Motto: Create proximity

Continuing with our puzzle-building analogy, when I'm thinking about what the end picture of my empowered church/organization should look like, I gather the people-puzzle pieces near me so I can see them. For me, creating proximity means I'm always looking for ways to be around and spend time with people in our congregation, our volunteers, and our staff. Each Sunday, I'm usually in the lobby interacting with volunteers and attendees. When I'm with people, I'm always trying to be aware of who they really are and their gifts and abilities. I'm also continually checking with the Holy Spirit to see if He has any ideas for me. Often, I'm right in the middle of a conversation with someone, and the thought comes into my mind about where the person would be most successful serving. At a recent Wednesday night service when I greeted a young man, I felt the Holy Spirit say, "This is the person you were praying about to add to your staff this morning."

I hired him at the end of that service, and he has been a superb addition to our team. At that same service, I was looking for a new volunteer-leader for a grocery distribution ministry. I shared the idea with a lady, and at that moment both of us knew she was the right fit. She was a proven leader with the call of God to minister to hurting people. The Holy Spirit makes my job so much easier! Most of our recruiting is for volunteers. As you well know, churches are truly run by volunteers. The ministry is a cooperative effort, and my goal in building an empowered organization is to release people to use the gifts of God in them to impact others. I'm continually finding a reason to interact with people and listening to the Holy Spirit to find out next steps for people, or where they might best use their talents in our body of believers.

Motto: I'm always connecting

The next step I'm trying to accomplish is to move and connect the people-pieces to general obvious areas. In puzzle building, I group like pieces together based on how they look: all the edge pieces together, the flowers, the mountains, sky, and trees, etc. Likewise, in building an empowerment culture, I start separating people into areas that are similar in purpose. If I happen to find two pieces that connect for a function, I put them together. But I'm continually looking at people and trying to discover their particular shape and how they will best combine. Finding the correct fit requires asking many questions, seeking answers about what things a person likes to do, what is important to them, and in what areas they have achieved success. I might ask what areas of ministry have stood out to them or resonated with them. "Do you like to sing? Are you musical? Maybe you could come to one of our worship team practices. Oh, you enjoy teenagers? Our youth group meets at six PM tonight. Why don't you check it out, and I will introduce you to the leader? Do you love to bake? Fantastic! Let me connect you to the gal that runs our hospitality ministry."

Developing a process to help people discover how they are wired is also beneficial. Once again, I believe this is why I was guided to write the book, *Well Done, Finding and Fulfilling God's Call on Your Life* several years ago. The book centers on the Parable of the Talents, in Matthew 25. It helps believers realize that we all have gifts/talents given to us by God and it is up to us to discover what they are, develop them, and use them for the Kingdom so we can achieve our ultimate goal of hearing from the Master, "Well done, thy good and faithful servant." The book has been a great tool and has been used extensively by individuals, in classes, small groups, and even Bible college to help people identify the call of God on their lives and take the next steps forward to fulfill it. There are also multiple personality tests, spiritual and natural gifting inventories, and other resources that people can use to hone their talents and how they might best put them to use in the Church.

Motto: Look to move people to their highest calling

Once I have gathered people into broad areas of evident giftings, I continue to observe their other attributes, which will determine their continued progression. Unlike puzzle pieces, people keep maturing and developing. They also have hidden talents I didn't realize they possess. I frequently put someone in a position and, as I'm observing them, I see further gifting which moves them again and again. This applies to both volunteers and paid staff.

It's important to mention that just because a person has some gifting in a particular area, doesn't necessarily mean that it will resonate with them in terms of a place of serving or ministry. Teachers are a great example of this point. We have many gifted educators in our congregations. Does that mean that every single one of them is serving in our children and youth ministries? Absolutely not! For some, the last thing they want to do on a Sunday morning is spend it with our precious children. Ha! And that's not a knock on them or on our kids. It just may not be an area of church ministry that fits for them. They spend their working hours ministering in their own way to children. But guess what? These are not "one talent" individuals like Servant #3 in the Parable of the Talents. If an apparent teaching ministry position doesn't fit, they find places within our church to use their musical talents, gifts of administration, encouragement, and on and on.

Motto: Proper pacing to promote

After the identification, sorting, and grouping processes have taken place in puzzle building, we start permanently locking pieces together as quickly as possible so we can see the picture they make. This isn't quite the case when I'm building an organization. Instead, I move at differing speeds at the connecting or hiring process. Initially, I'm usually pretty quick to get someone moved to a general area of interest. "You look like a rock. Let me get you in the general area of other rocks." However, before I commit for them to be a leader or to hire them, it might take several years for me to observe their character and abilities. I like to reflect on their strengths, dependability, and other characteristics to make a proper decision. I know this is a business concept, but I'm continually looking at the risk of placing a person in a position and the return they will bring. If I know them, have worked well with them for years, and I've received the Holy Spirit's approval, it markedly reduces the risk of a wrong decision.

Motto: Create a culture of open communication

Wouldn't it be great if while we were building a puzzle, the pieces helped? What if they could talk and say, "Hey, I'm a rock. I know I may not look like it, but I fit in with the other rocks in the river. Why don't you put me over there?" Yep, that would be a huge advantage. Truthfully, I don't want the pressure of trying to be everyone's holy spirit, with them waiting for me to hear from God and place them in an area or ministry. That's too much pressure. I try to create an atmosphere and a culture for people to grow and develop, but I ultimately want their feedback on where they think they should be. I can't read minds, and I don't know what God has placed on their heart. I don't know what their passions and compassions are, and I want their input so, together, we can find the right place for them to flourish for the Kingdom. To get this vital information from them, we need to create a culture of communication and feedback. I want to know what they are praying about and believing for God to help them accomplish. Sometimes God does speak to me about individuals who should move forward. That said, ultimately it is up to each individual to find and fulfill their place in the Kingdom. It is up to me to create an open, empowering atmosphere for them to achieve this. There also needs to be a real sense of freedom, where people can take a step and try a ministry or area. If one area doesn't work, then they will feel comfortable trying something else until it is a match made in heaven. Sometimes it takes trying a few areas to find a good fit. That's okay because the main thing is that they move to the spot where they need to be to fulfill the call of God on their life.

Baby Whisperer, or Not

My wife, Dianne, is an amazing mother. She had six children, and each one has been a joy to her. I call Dianne a "baby whisperer" because of her love and patience for children. She has a natural sense of what they need and exactly how to relate to them. Watching her interact with a baby is like a master conductor or painter; it is just beautiful. When Dianne was seeking to find the call of God on her life, it seemed so obvious that she should work in the church nursery. What is interesting is that Dianne volunteered one week in the nursery, and she just sensed that wasn't where God wanted her to be. Inside, she desired to help ladies and lead a women's Bible study. So she gradually gave that a go.

Failing to Success

To say Dianne's initial results in leading a women's Bible study were dismal would be an understatement. For her first year, she essentially had one lady who consistently attended. The attendee was an elderly lady who was lonely and couldn't drive. She said if Dianne would drive across town, pick her up, drive her to the church where they met, then drive her back home (possibly run a few errands on the way and go out to lunch), she would attend. After that first year, I asked Dianne what she thought, and she said, "You know, things haven't gone very well, but I think I'm supposed to continue." And she did. Dianne kept learning, growing, praying, and persisting. Her faithfulness has paid off because as of this writing, Dianne has the largest, most successful "small" group in our church. The group has grown so much they need a large room and a sound system! The ladies are so adamant about attending they won't consider taking any breaks throughout the year for holidays or the summer. But the best part of all is the results we see coming from this group. When these women pray, people get saved, lives are changed, and people are healed from sicknesses. They are a powerful force for the Kingdom!

Church Advantage

In building an empowerment culture, the Church has an enormous advantage over businesses. First off, there is no higher calling than doing Kingdom work. Nothing compares! If we can't create a compelling vision for people to identify the call of God on their life and the ability to fulfill it, we don't have a clear grasp of what we are called to do as church leaders. There is no greater honor than to use the gifts God Himself gave us to further His Kingdom. It just doesn't get any better than that!

Motto: Develop a farm team

The second advantage when it comes to the leadership of the church is that we have a huge volunteer base. If handled correctly, these volunteers can develop into an excellent leadership pipeline for future organizational success. Let's take the example of baseball. Baseball has what are called farm teams. "Farm Team" is a general metaphor for any organization that serves as a training ground for higher-level performance. Think of the pipeline that supports the baseball industry. Millions of children start in tee-ball every year, graduating to coach pitch, a pitching machine, and eventually playing fast-pitch. Baseball has an extensive system of high school, college, all-star teams, semi-pro teams, all the way to the pros. The individual steps aren't important. What is essential is a system of training to develop a person from the entry level, where they don't know what a baseball is or which way to run the bases, to the elite athlete playing in the Major Leagues. We can develop a very similar system in churches. Just like with baseball, most people aren't paid until they develop some proficiency in their abilities. Baseball would go broke if they had to pay kids learning how to play tee-ball; however, they gladly pay people who make it to the pros. Most businesses don't have a large volunteer contingency from which they can develop and hire people. However, access to a large volunteer base is a standard operating procedure in the church and nonprofit world.

As an empowerment leader in a church or organization, I know I will need leaders in one year, three years, five years, and beyond. Why not develop an ongoing system where new leaders will be plentiful for future growth?

Built into volunteer positions is a system for growth, feedback, and increased responsibility. A person may enter the children's ministry as a once-a-month volunteer in the nursery. After several months of rocking babies, this volunteer, let's call her Anne, decides that she is better suited to working with older children, so she moves to the preschool department. After serving as a helper with the three- and four-year-olds for a year, Anne has been trained and shown herself as dependable and confirmed her giftings. She has developed her ability, and the department head encourages her to take the role of a teacher. Anne knows the leadership believes in promoting people based on their skills and their faithfulness, so after praying about it, she accepts the position. Fast forward a few years later, Anne is still happily teaching in the preschool department; however, she has been promoted again to the department head, encouraging others to develop their abilities and step forward. She is now part of the paid part-time staff, working on developing an innovative curriculum for kiddos, and leading quarterly training sessions for new teachers and volunteers in the children's ministry. Anne has worked her way up to playing in the big leagues now!

Motto: Everyone replaces themselves

A significant element of an empowerment culture should be for each person who serves, whether they are a volunteer or paid staff, to have the perspective they should be training someone to replace them. There are several reasons why this is such a powerful concept, both for the individual to move up and for the health of the organization. First, a person shows their leadership if they are training their replacements; this is also how they are elevated in an organization. It is an enormous benefit for me to see people raising up other people behind them. Not only are they showing how responsible they are by discipling someone, but they are making my job easier as well.

Training our replacement is also healthier for the organization. Eventually, we'll all leave the position or job we have, whether we are promoted, move, or retire. It should be our heart's desire that our area is fully covered by a knowledgeable, forward-thinking replacement to ensure a smooth transition. This is good stewardship. On the practical side, we don't always know when God is going to call us to another location or organization, so we should have our designated replacement-in-training ready to take over for us. Each person, when asked, should be able to say "_______ is who I'm training to be my replacement."

My office staff knows that if ever they were to leave our organization, it is their responsibility to replace themselves. Why? The answer is easy; that is what love would do. It is my goal to walk in love toward my staff, and that they reciprocate by walking in love toward me. If ever we need to part ways, it is my goal to do it in a loving, caring manner, with me helping them move forward, and them making for a smooth replacement transition. If I ever have a person that gives me a two-week notice and they have not trained their replacement, I know I have failed in helping that person to understand our culture, because love does not act that way.

Let me give you an example of reciprocating walking in love when one person moves on from a job. This situation confirmed we were on the right path of creating a healthy culture of caring about each other on our staff.[3] [4] There was a young lady in our office who, among other things, handled my travel arrangements. She was very good at it, but things changed in our office, and we no longer needed her on a full-time basis. I talked with her, and we parted ways on good terms. I tried to do everything I could to help her with her job relocation. Several months later, when she was no longer on the staff, and I hadn't been in contact with her, she called me out of the blue and said, "Mac, I heard you have an upcoming trip; if you run into any travel difficulties I'm available and just a phone call away to work out any situations for you."

That's what love does.

Motto: Recruit and hire based on the Four Cs

There are four general Cs for me to consider when examining puzzle-piece shapes and organizational fit, beyond their primary function. The four Cs are: Character, Calling, Capability, and Culture. All of these are equally important. Think of these four Cs as spokes on a wheel. If one of the spokes is undersized, we are in for a very bumpy ride together. When looking for leaders (either staff or department heads of various ministries), I like to have people who are high in character, working in their life calling or gifting, highly capable of accomplishing things relative to their position, and a match for our organizational culture. If they are not high in all these traits, I know it is going to create friction and problems. Being lopsided doesn't disqualify people. We are all growing in different areas. I know that I need to put those who have "lopsided spokes" in an environment where they can grow, and then I continually observe how they are progressing. I'm always looking long range, wanting to have people engaged in building the next generation of leaders. It makes sense to take a more in-depth look at these attributes.

Character

In the church world, we would all think that a self-evident virtue would be a person of integrity. On the other hand, we have all seen people who have been elevated due to their capabilities but were later removed because their character could not sustain where their gifting took them. I have made a list of personal attributes and prioritized them based on my reflections. For our church, the following characteristics are vital to our success: Honesty, Loyalty, Communication, and Initiative. I would recommend you do the same, regarding what is important to you for your team culture.

Calling

It is imperative for people to work in a position where God has given them gifts and abilities. Ultimately, I would like them so passionate about fulfilling the call of God, they can't imagine *not* doing it. As a reminder, the call on people's lives is where people are graced by God to succeed; it is the release of the God Pod abilities placed in them. My prayer for them is that they discover their calling and it becomes a burning passion for them. I hope they come to a place where they believe, "This is the call of God on my life, and I have to fulfill it. It is my life mission." I probably won't have people start out this way, but it is a great place to grow toward.

Capability

A relatively easy thing to determine is a person's capabilities, or is it? Because most people are multi-talented, it is sometimes easy to overlook complementary or secondary giftings that can be very valuable to the Kingdom. Often, I connect with someone based on a skill set they have. As I begin working with them, I find additional skills and knowledge that makes them even more valuable to me, and for Kingdom growth. "Oh, I didn't know you had a knack for social media, technology, etc. Wow, I'm glad we have been working together. Are you open to some other ideas on how we could use your skills?" The earlier principles of proximity and moving people to their highest calling come into play when evaluating someone's capabilities.

Culture

Culture is another thing that might not seem all that important in the team-building process, but if you hire a person of high character and capabilities, and they don't believe in what you are doing or agree with your spiritual values, this can be a recipe for turmoil. Maybe they don't have the same work ethic. Maybe there is nothing ethically wrong with these people; they just think they are superior to everyone else or perhaps they are not good teammates. It could be that they cause continual frustration and division. You have heard the saying, "A rotten apple spoils the whole bunch," and it is true. If you have a person with a sour disposition or who does not fit into your culture, it is just not worth the harm they can bring to others on your team. Someone else might be a lot of fun to be around but accomplish very little, leaving others to pick up the slack. These are all signs of a bad cultural fit. If these people don't fit into your culture, they can cause you to lose high-capacity workers because they won't tolerate the atmosphere that the problematic person is creating, or they resent having to cover for the lack of productivity from the other. I heard one leader say they only hire people who give them energy and those who they feel good working alongside. I agree. I like to hire people who are pleasant to be around, hardworking, as well as forward-thinking. In team building, the healthy team culture is incredibly important for success.

Motto: Through prayer and observation, hire the best

Hiring the right team members is crucial to success, so it's imperative that we take our time. Maybe it's just me, but if I'm hiring a receptionist, it may take me six months to find exactly the right person. Usually, I'm trying to hire someone that is gifted well beyond the primary duties of a receptionist. I approach this situation by getting them in our proximity to determine what they can do and start developing them for another position. Is this what most churches do? Maybe not. It is interesting to me that if I post an employment ad, I may hear, "You should hire Martha. She is out of work. She could really use the money. I'm sure she could answer the phones for you." Here is the thing; I want the best for Martha, and if she is the right fit for us and we are the right fit for her, excellent! Come aboard, Martha! However, I'm building the highest caliber Jesus Team possible to accomplish great things for the Kingdom, and I want the highest quality, most capable leaders I can find.

I have the viewpoint that if I have to tell people what to do, I probably hired the wrong people or have them in the wrong spot. I expect people to be self-starters, have initiative and they should be problem-solving and building their own job description. They should be continually refining what needs to be done to move the organization to our goal, mission or vision. I want to work with mature, hardworking self-driven people that will manage their behaviors to get us to a successful result. Hiring the right people with a high level of wisdom and initiative means I don't have to manage them; they naturally self-correct for continued growth.

I have a limited amount of time on this earth, and I want to have the most excellent results for the Kingdom that I can achieve. Through prayer, I hire the most talented people I can. It just makes my life easier. At one time I had a small ranch with horses, and there was a saying, "It costs just as much to feed a good horse as it does a bad horse." I want to fill my stable with thoroughbreds that want to win the Kingdom race.

Motto: Coach in the moment

In real life, most people-puzzle pieces don't fit neatly into the final picture without some refinements. Think of the analogy of the potter and the clay; we all need to be refined to be better used for the Master's work. I know I need to grow and be refined continually, and it appears others may as well. I want people to develop and improve at their own pace. This is where our farm-team, growth-oriented volunteer base comes into play. I try to encourage people to move forward, but the bottom line is, when I am looking for leaders, I want to work with people who take the initiative to step up and solve problems. I love it when people see a problem, and they take action to address it appropriately. When people take the initiative, sometimes things don't work out; that is a natural consequence of an empowerment culture. It is okay when they make mistakes because I can lovingly train them in the moment. "Hey, I love your eagerness to solve that problem. Let's talk through what didn't work as we had hoped." Within this process, I'm like a coach, and I want to give feedback in the moment. Isn't that what great coaches do? A great football coach doesn't say, "Last week when you went to make that one block you were at the wrong angle." The player wouldn't learn anything. I use this process anytime we have major events as well. I like to gather the team together right afterward and talk through all the things they did right to reinforce what is working. I also politely let them know where we can do better. Usually, if I need to bring correction, I do it privately, and I praise people publicly. The reason we give praise openly is that it lets everyone know what things we value.

Motto: Recruit people with high initiative

There is a saying that water always seeks its own level. No, this witty saying is not a Bible verse; it's a scientific fact. What does this mean to us in building empowered teams? For empowered people to succeed, it is up to us to remove obstacles and create an environment where people can promote themselves based on their initiative and competence. This takes immense pressure off leadership because I don't have to give promotions. I look for people who have abilities and take the initiative for the overall success and wellbeing of the organization. It is easy for me to observe people's behaviors. This works equally with volunteers or paid staff. Are they hard working, diligent, have great attitudes, and do they follow through? Do they take action to complete tasks and find ways to make things better and create improvements? Are they training others and replacing themselves? If they are, they are rising in the organization. If they are not, well, it's okay because they are on the farm team for the future. If I have developed a healthy environment, others will grow now and fill in that space of success. It is up to me to get the right, innovative people in proximity and create an environment for their success. It is up to the individual to take the initiative in utilizing their abilities. This way I don't have to promote people; they promote themselves. Water seeks its own level, and your people will too if you create the environment for them to rise to their level of success freely.

In an empowerment culture, how do people get promoted? They advance themselves by accomplishing past their present position. You might be thinking, what if my hard efforts aren't appreciated and rewarded by being promoted? First, we are all working for God, and He is the rewarder. Also, I know if I do not acknowledge and compensate people adequately, they will leave and rise in someone else's organization. Water will seek its own level and so will people. I would rather have people succeed in my organization than in someone else's.

Motto: Discipleship comes through working together

Gradually, create a system where your people-puzzle pieces can grow and develop to their full potential. Back to our baseball analogy, people progress best when they are in the game. How would it work out if tee-ballers spent hours in a classroom learning about baseball, but not being able to play the game? I think the number of players would fall substantially. Should there be teaching? Sure, but discipleship comes through getting in the game, through serving. Let's look at how Jesus discipled the twelve. They would walk and talk. He would walk up to a fig tree, curse it, and later debrief on what happened (Mark 11:12-25). He would teach and feed the crowds, and then later discuss with his disciples the deeper meaning of what had just happened (Mark 8:1-21). Jesus coached in the moment; He did not wait until the disciples' annual work review to give them feedback. "Peter, remember when you tried to walk on water six months ago, and you thought you might drown...here are my thoughts." I don't think so! Give people constructive, hopefully encouraging feedback in the moment, creating a system that disciples them through connection with other believers so they will continue to progress in their giftings and life as well.

Motto: The greenhouse effect

We have talked about creating an environment for people to grow at their own pace. This is a crucial requirement for success because people, like plants, develop at different times and rates. Some people accept Jesus and immediately are in hot pursuit of their destiny. Others seem to be in hibernation mode for years and then one day, they hear a particular sermon, or a life-changing event happens and bang, they take off serving God. It is my job to create a greenhouse effect where everyone is welcome in a warm, accepting environment. This atmosphere is non-judgmental but encourages people to grow, change, and discover their life mission. It gives them the necessary resources and encouragement to go forth and accomplish it. As a leader, it is up to me to create this healthy climate where people are placed around other growing, striving people who are maturing. The power of association with our earlier popcorn analogy will help seemingly lifeless people pop into their Kingdom success.

DECISION MAKING FOR EMPOWERMENT

Before we close out this chapter, let me take a moment to discuss the decision-making process when it comes to empowering people within the organization, whether they are paid staff or volunteers.

Track record of individual or leader

There are a number of factors that come into play when deciding how to empower individuals. Some of the first things to look at are who is asking, what is their track record, and what is the rationale behind the decision they want to make. Are they experienced? Do they have the necessary knowledge or expertise to carry out what they are going to attempt?

Risk & Return

What is the risk in the decision? Is there a risk of money, time, or manpower? What resources are we committing to do this? Is there a long-term commitment? What is the downside if everything goes wrong? How visible would the mistake be? What is the win if we try? Many times, I let people try things even if I don't think they will work. My rationale is there is very little risk, and they will learn through the process. I have also wanted to try things because I knew they wouldn't work, but on the other side, I could demonstrate to the team that it is safe to try new things and there are no negative consequences. I want to teach and set an example to the whole team that it is encouraged and safe to come up with new ideas.

Scalability

One of the next questions I want to ask is, "Is it scalable?" Scalable growth is growth that can be scaled and sustained without a negative impact on the quality of your services. Scalable growth is sustainable, scalable, and predictable, without any effect on your creative output.

Will something that works for a church of a hundred people also work for a church of ten thousand people? What is the ongoing feasibility of time, money, and human resources necessary to accomplish the desired outcome? If the senior pastor of a very small church sees the potential for growth and commits to taking all new people to lunch, this will help them grow. However, how does that work or scale with a church of 10,000 and hundreds of new families each week? If our idea works or is necessary for success, how do we scale it to larger proportions including time, money, manpower, facilities, etc.?

Duplicatable

Along with scalability, I want to look at whether or not we are setting a precedent with this decision. Is this a one-time thing, or are we setting a pattern that everyone will expect from now on? Will this idea work just for us and this situation, or can other people or churches use the idea? An example of duplication is a franchised business. The concept works once, and we can duplicate the business in other cities. Scalability also comes into play when deciding if something is duplicatable. Yes, we may be able to duplicate the idea, but if every store costs one million dollars to open, it greatly effects how fast we can expand.

I hope it has been beneficial for you to have more concrete information on what empowerment is and how to implement it. The principles in this chapter are things I continue to reflect on while making decisions to build an empowerment culture. I know that if I will keep them in mind and continually tune in to the wisdom and direction of the Holy Spirit, things seem to have a way of working out. Most of these principles can be implemented slowly. I start making decisions, and then I describe the motto that helped me make that determination to the people involved in that specific situation. This helps in the discipleship process of mentoring people on how to make decisions. Next, we are going to cover some additional empowerment thoughts that are critical to functioning in a healthy manner for maximum results.

Chapter 11 Reflection Questions

1. What are ways that you can create proximity with people in your organization?

2. What are some ways that you can foster open communication as people move into positions of serving and leadership?

3. What systems do you have in place for people to discover their gifts and talents?

4. How are you developing your farm team?

5. What characteristics in leaders are vital for your organization's success? What are your top four cultural values?

Chapter 12: Empowerment Thoughts

Empowerment Accountability

When individuals hear about an empowerment culture, their immediate response can be, "Yes! That is what I want! I'm tired of being restricted or micromanaged and want to be free to make decisions without consulting anyone." While I'm generally glad they feel like they want to take the initiative and be part of moving things forward, there is a greater responsibility and accountability that comes with being empowered. When we are an empowered leader, we are held to a higher level of accountability in the area we have stewardship over. The more empowered we are, the more accountability and responsibility we have. Jesus made this point in the parable of the steward who was made ruler over his master's household, noting that the one who knew his master's will would be held more accountable than those who didn't. "...For everyone to whom much is given, from him much will be required; and to whom much has been committed, of him they will ask the more." (Luke 12:42-48 NKJV) Being empowered is a very humbling and serious assignment. If we truly understand the reality of empowerment, it can be very intimidating. We should be praying, studying, and growing more than ever, seeking the Holy Spirit's wisdom and guidance. In this position, we have become responsible for the outcome of our area of stewardship, and that outcome affects individual people and possibly the entire organization. This is the sobering reality about being empowered leadership, and it should not be taken lightly, but instead, we should embrace the position as if we're doing it unto the Lord.

Since we, as empowered leaders, are responsible for the outcome of our area of stewardship, there must be a way to measure our effectiveness. We see the example of this in the Parable of the Talents. Each steward received a certain number of talents based on his ability. Each steward was accountable and held responsible for what they did with what they were given when their Master came back (Matthew 25:14-30). In an empowerment culture, we measure results based on predetermined goals or metrics, which are numbers we track to a specific outcome. Some examples of these goals or metrics might be attendance, the number of people in your small group, the total of new attendees, or the increase in outreach ministries, etc. The outcomes or metrics track part of the empowered leader's effectiveness. Some desired results are harder to quantify, but we should endeavor to do so. Since empowerment and accountability are connected, there must be a way for us to measure a person or group's empowerment results. We should strive to establish goals or outcomes for all the areas of our organization, and then give increased empowerment to those who have attained the predetermined results.

Committed to Communicate

Many people want to have an empowerment culture, but there are responsibilities involved with having a strong, empowered team. The most important commitment is communication for all parties involved in the empowerment process. Let's talk about why communication is so important.

Communication is a two-way street. Leadership *must* be committed to sharing dreams, visions, core values, metrics, and all pertinent information for teammates to make good decisions. If we, as leaders, are expecting people to have sound judgment, we must be open with our thoughts and the rationale behind organizational decisions and actions. When I started my first company at 18, I was in way over my head and clueless about how to run a business, including the myriad of decisions I was called to make. To avoid getting overwhelmed I used to tell myself, "Mac, you can make any decision if you have enough information." When I had gathered all the pertinent data, most decisions were easy because, with all the information, the best choice was apparent. As empowerment leaders, we want our teammates to make quality decisions, so we need to furnish them with all the related pieces of information and encourage their additional research to help in their decision-making process. If we don't inform them, and they make a wrong decision, we could be the ultimate cause of the poor outcome because we did not adequately communicate all our thoughts or insights.

In an empowerment culture, teams also need to communicate with leadership. Remember, this is a two-way street. It's unfortunate, but I have been guilty of placing my pastor and his wife in very uncomfortable situations because I had not informed them of a decision I had made. Could you imagine being the senior pastor and people in the congregation knowing things that are going on and decisions that were made and you don't? I put them in an awkward position because I had not done an acceptable job of communicating with them. Other times I have had staff make decisions that ended up as dismal failures. If they had checked with me first or told me what they were working on, I could have saved them considerable grief. Because of my prior experience or understanding, I had already made or seen those same mistakes. I could have helped them avoid those unnecessary pitfalls. There is a principle that says, "We should never try something new without talking to our leadership." Chances are leadership has already tried it, knows someone who has, or can give reflections on the validity of the idea. Their experience and knowledge can often save time, money, frustration, and in some instances, embarrassment. Leadership and empowered teams must commit to communicating. Communication doesn't happen just once, but it is an endless chain of dialogue, including verbal, e-mails, texts, memos, etc.

Vision for Empowerment

In addition to communication, empowerment leadership takes vision. A common question I get asked is, "Mac, much of what you talk about requires me as a leader being a visionary or speaking a vision. I'm not a natural visionary nor am I good at creating a vision, so how do I do it?" I appreciate the honesty. Vision applies to all areas of leadership, whether you are a pastor, corporate leader, ministry leader, small group leader, or head of a family. If even one person is looking to us, we need to be able to create a picture of where we are going. Yes, some people create a vision more easily than others. I'm one of those people. It is hard for me *not* to talk about moving forward to a more successful outcome. Hopefully, this book is helping you picture vibrant, functioning teams of people taking ownership, responsibility, and initiative, which results in a flourishing organization.

I think many people make creating a vision too hard and complicated. Here are some tips.

1. Peer into the future and describe what it would generally look like. Be clear about what you are trying to achieve.

2. Break that down and define the next steps of the foreseeable future, not 80 years from now. Setting strategic goals brings a sense of reality to the vision.

3. Set measurable and specific goals, so your team knows when they have hit the target.[1]

4. Describe the results of a healthy, thriving church or organization.

5. Keep communicating the vision and sharing information.[2]

6. You may want to avoid the trap of putting hard numbers or dates to the vision. Too many things can alter a timed goal.

Examples of Vision Sentences

Even though I'm asking a question, it is a safe, easy way to move people's minds to start visualizing outcomes.

Here are some great first words and complementary ideas to help you describe a vision:

1. **What if**...we had outreach ministries serving people all over our city?

2. **Let's imagine**...new church campuses bringing God's goodness throughout our state.

3. **Let's think about**...what it would be like with our church impacting our community.

4. **Let's picture**...what our church would be like with everyone avidly seeking the will of God for their life.

5. **Let's think about**...us working together as a team; what could we accomplish in this ministry?

6. **What would**...our children's ministry be like if we were the example for all other children's ministries? What would it look like? What attributes would it have? What would the impact be on children and families?

Notice that we are letting people imagine the individual picture in their mind. Everyone will have a slightly different image as it relates to them. The more we talk and create the vision, the clearer it becomes. Creating this image for our people is a *requirement* for leaders. Research shows that "Employees who find their company's vision meaningful have engagement levels of 68 percent, which is 19 points above average. More engaged employees are often more productive, and they are more effective corporate ambassadors in the larger community."[3] Do you think these figures are similar for church volunteers? Most likely. If we do not create a vision, people will create their own, or more likely, wander away to some place where there is clear direction. The Bible says, "[W]here there is no vision, the people perish..." (Proverbs 29:18 KJV). I believe that is why the Dones have left the Church and the younger generation is not drawn to it; there is no clear mission. People are attracted to vision. Either we will provide this direction, or the world will.

As leaders, the excuse that God has not given us a vision or told us what to do won't work. The Bible gives us God's purpose for humanity when it says, "...God our Savior, who desires all men to be saved and to come to the knowledge of the truth" (1 Timothy 2:3b-4 NKJV). And what is that knowledge of the truth? You see it on poster boards at ball games all the time. Good ol' John 3:16. "For God so loved the world that He gave His only begotten Son, that whoever believes in Him should not perish but have everlasting life." (NKJV) Additionally, the Bible is full of mandates to get us moving forward. We are told to make disciples of all nations, feed the hungry, etc.

There is a multitude of things we are clearly directed to do. Saying we don't have a vision can be an excuse because either we are too lazy to develop one, or we don't want to put in the effort to equip people properly to fulfill it. It's okay to have a small objective, as long as it's moving people forward. Once we speak the mission out, we need to help people facilitate it. So if we say, "Let's picture a growing, thriving church with amazing worship and great services that people would want to attend and bring their friends along," this is an easily perceptible vision. What would that be like? There may need to be a fair amount of change to accomplish this result, but we are heading in the right direction by getting people to conceptualize robust growth.

Too Much Vision

Some people are on the opposite side of the spectrum and they are too visionary. Say what? How is that possible? The vision they speak out may be so broad that people can't relate to it, or they might change the focus every week. One week they are talking about starting small groups on every street in their city, the next week opening church campuses in every town in the nation, and the following week they are launching the first church on Mars. People become confused, and their energies aren't directed toward accomplishing anything.

Speak the Vision All the Time

If we are serious about achieving our vision, we must speak some form of it all the time. The Lord told us to "Write the vision and make it plain...that he may run who reads it." (Habakkuk 2:2) Write it and then speak it. This means that every Sunday people should hear a core value, testimony, statement, etc. about where you as a church or organization are going. There should be posters, specific sermons, teachings, classes, banners, and flyers all saying the same thing: "This is where we are going, and we are facilitating and training people to get there." If you are not a natural visionary, have people help. Communicate with your team and enlist their help to create a way to share these objectives more clearly.

A Vision for Well Done

The Biblical example and directive to hear, "Well done," is an incredibly powerful catalyst to create the vision within an empowerment culture. We have noted that from a Biblical perspective, hearing, "Well done," from our Lord is the ultimate accomplishment that we should be aspiring to hear. Painting the picture of standing before the judgment seat of God and hearing, "Well done," is a great visual tool to help us move every person forward, creating both a personal vision and an end goal for their life. If people within an empowerment culture have a vision to hear, "Well done," great things can happen.

In an effort to foster the vision, we continually talk to people about the importance of hearing, "Well done," placing this goal in the forefront of people's minds. This, in turn, allows the Holy Spirit the opportunity to lead them to natural next steps and empower them to accomplish them. As a result, people might start saying, "Oh, I feel like I need to enroll in Bible college, start a home Bible study, get on a Bible reading plan, read a book on ministry, or subscribe to a podcast on leadership." This happens because you helped them visualize the ultimate biblical outcome of Jesus standing before them, looking into their eyes, and saying, "Well done, thou good and faithful servant." Isn't that what every leader would want for their congregation or followers? If you had a church or organization full of people focused on developing and applying themselves for the unmatched outcome of hearing, "Well done," what would happen? Do you think people would be making every effort to achieve more, studying and developing in their off hours? Do you think your team would get along better and be happier? Do you believe it would result in lower turnover because your team knows their ultimate destination, and that you care enough about them to help them get there? Do you think there would be more production and success? Would everything be better and happier because you helped other people succeed first?

Tenets of Empowerment

As previously discussed, empowerment is a powerful concept, but it can seem abstract. Below, I have attempted to create a table to help us understand the relationship between the "empowerer" and the "empowered" and the responsibilities of each. First, leadership or the "empowerer" speaks the vision—the goal the team is aiming for. We have already talked about tips for speaking and clarifying a vision. The empowered person or teams should listen, hear, understand, and receive the vision. Next, the parties agree on a step or outcomes that will move the organization closer to attaining the end goal. It is up to leadership to accurately communicate all applicable information so the empowered team can achieve it. This is where I often see leadership dropping the ball.

Many times, when I observe a team making a mistake, it is connected back to leadership not sharing vital decision-making information for the successful outcome. The parties agree on the **what** (goal) that is to be accomplished, and there is flexibility in the **how** it can get done. Leaving the **how** flexible can lead the team to exciting innovative breakthroughs. There needs to be regular feedback by both parties, which means the "how" should be communicated back to leadership. Once the event or time frame is complete, the results are analyzed by both parties. Part of this process involves discussing and asking questions about what worked and what did not. Asking questions is beneficial to help us have more understanding as we plan the next steps to move forward. When we accomplish our outcomes, goals, or objectives it is imperative to stop and purposely celebrate the victories that are moving us closer to our ultimate vision. This creates continual energy toward success. After we critique and learn from our last process and have celebrated our success, we agree again on the next outcome and repeat the process to the ultimate accomplishment of the vision!

Empowerer	Empowered
Speaks the vision.	**Hears and embraces the vision.**
• Gives authority and power.	• Receive authority, power, accountability and responsibility.
• Parties agree on the "what" of *outcomes or goals to move toward the vision.	• Agree on the "what" of *outcomes or goals to move toward the vision.
• Communicates necessary information for decision making including: vision, core values and all needed information.	• Find the "how" to accomplish the "what" by prayer, research and due diligence.
• Support the efforts of the empowered team.	• Communicate how they will accomplish the what of outcomes.
• Review the results.	• Accomplish and review the results.
• Celebrate the successful accomplishment!	• Celebrate the successful accomplishment!
• Learn from process.	• Learn from process.
• Plan the next outcome.	• Plan the next outcome.
• Repeat the process.	• Repeat the process.
**Outcomes:* * Metrics * Value	

Closing Empowerment Thoughts

The above narrative and table are guidelines to help you develop the processes of an empowered culture. The template works with a variety of sizes of teams or organizations. Feel free to adapt and change the process to what works best for you.

Remember the "what" is to develop an empowerment culture. The "how" is up to you and your team to create a functioning system so ultimately your victories can be celebrated. The implementation of empowerment may take some time and refinements. As you and your team continue, you will be able to modify and decide what works best for you to accomplish your goals.

I talk about empowerment as a powerful means to release the God pod abilities of people to build a thriving church, and it is. I do want to bring some balance to the subject because it can come across that in an empowerment culture, people are continually taking the initiative, resulting constant change. This is not the case. We do want to empower people to solve problems, but then we standardize the solution. Let's think about the fast-food industry. Over the years people have been empowered to find the best processes to produce a product the consumer wants. The system is highly standardized so teenagers can become a valuable part of operating a multi-million dollar business. Standardized procedures provide an exact road map and game plan of what to do for a successful outcome. Empower gifted people to develop a process that creates the intended result. Keep asking questions regarding what is working and why and continue to refine the system for greater impact in changing lives for the Kingdom.

We have covered a lot of ground in this relatively short book; that is why most people will find it handy to keep it as a reference, reread it, and use it as a resource they can discuss and give away to others for mutual success. In the next chapter, I want to share some personal reflections that will hopefully enhance and continue our journey of empowering people to hear, "Well done."

Chapter 12 Reflection Questions

1. What is the relationship between empowerment and accountability?

2. What are some metrics that you can use to track the effectiveness of empowerment in your organization?

3. How can you facilitate increased communication between leadership and teams and vice versa in your organization?

4. What is your vision for your area of leadership?

5. Have you effectively communicated that vision, and do you do so regularly? If not, what are some things that you can implement to share your vision?

6. Can you think of other leaders who might benefit from the insights in this book?

[1] https://magazine.vunela.com/4-steps-to-creating-a-shared-vision-that-will-energize-your-team-82b801e742ed/accessed 03/21/201

[2] https://www.recruiter.com/i/3-steps-to-establishing-a-shared-vision-of-success-for-your-organization/accessed 03/21/2019

[3] https://www.businessnewsdaily.com/3882-vision-statement.html accessed 03/23/2019

[4] https://en.wikipedia.org/wiki/Jim_Elliot accessed 03/25/2019

Chapter 13: A New Beginning

Growth, whether it's personal or organizational, can bring on numerous emotions. It can be exciting to see your vision start to manifest, it can be confusing when things don't go as expected, or even downright painful when you are stretched beyond your comfort zone. Most of us have heard the saying, "To get something you never had, you have to do something you never did." God wants us to move beyond our comfort zones while listening to His voice and trusting that the vision He has given each one of us will come to pass if we follow His leading.

This "walking by faith and not by sight" (2 Corinthians 5:7) concept can be seen in one of my favorite Bible adventures, the story of Jonathan and his armor-bearer in 1 Samuel 14. I'll give you the summarized version, relieving you of the daunting task of sounding out all the places and names. Unless you want to practice your Hebrew? Maybe another time.

So, the Israelites and the Philistines were at war with one another, with their armies camped on either side of the valley. Jonathan, the son of the King of Israel, instructed his armor-bearer, "Come, let us go over to the Philistines' garrison that is on the other side." (vs.1) So they snuck off, just the two of them, without telling the king.

There were some sharp rocks they had to scale to get to the Philistines' camp, but Jonathan didn't seem phased by such perilous terrain. He had vision. Instead, he commanded his armor-bearer, "Come, let us go over to the garrison of these uncircumcised; it may be that the Lord will work for us. For nothing restrains the Lord from saving by many or by few." (vs.6) Then the armor-bearer replied, "Do all that is in your heart. Go then; here I am with you, according to your heart." (vs.7)

So Jonathan made a plan. They would show themselves to the Philistines as they were climbing. If the Philistines told them to wait until they came down to Jonathan and his man, the two men wouldn't climb up to them. However, if the Philistines told them to climb up to them, then the two men would continue to climb up because that would be the sign that the Lord would help them defeat the Philistines. (vss.8-10)

When Jonathan and his armor-bearer showed themselves, the Philistines told them to come up to them. Jonathan took that as confirmation of their impending victory as he confidently instructed his armor-bearer, "Come up after me, for the Lord has delivered them into the hand of Israel." (vs.12b)

Sure enough, as Jonathan climbed up, their enemies fell before him, and he and his armor-bearer killed all 20 men. This was followed by an earthquake that made the Philistine army tremble and flee, and Israel was saved. (vss.14-23)

Can't you just picture this as a scene in the comedic parody movie, Monty Python and the Holy Grail? "Hey what do you think about you and me taking on a garrison of Philistine soldiers?" His loyal subject responds in kind, "Oh, that's a great idea. Let's do it!" But that's just the beginning because Jonathan comes up with another brilliant idea. "We will let the garrison see the two of us, and if they say come up here, that will be our sign to go up and fight." Some people might see this as just a tad reckless. Obviously, the Holy Spirit was involved with this amazing encounter. The Holy Spirit had apparently been placing thoughts in Jonathan's mind about the possibilities, giving him a vision. This is very similar to how I see my relationship with the Holy Spirit. I feel like I'm the armor-bearer and my buddy, the Holy Spirit, is saying, "Hey, Mac! I have this idea. You want to do it?" I always want my response to be, "Wow, of course I do! That sounds like an amazing idea."

Why do I tell you this story? What if the Holy Spirit is saying to you and me, "Hey, do you want to do something amazing? Do you want to see the Body of Christ resurrect and terror spread through the enemy ranks?" The world sees us as a small group of weak people, cowardly hanging out together at our (church) camp. Do you want to do something exciting that will make the whole world tremble? What if we release and empower the abilities of the people in our camps? What if we united on common ground the way Jesus instructed? What if we took the guidance of our Counselor, the Holy Spirit? Soon the enemy armies would be fleeing. It is up to each one of us to hear the Holy Spirit's directions and take the next step forward of releasing the God Pod abilities bottled up on the inside of us, uniting with other God-gifted people to accomplish great and wonderful things for the Kingdom of God. When we do this, we can hear the ultimate accolade, "Well done, thou good and faithful servant." This brings me to my secret prayer, and since we are friends, I'm going to risk sharing it with you.

Just This Planet

Since we have traveled this far together, I feel I can be transparent and share with you a very secret, heartfelt prayer I sometimes pray. Before the prayer, I start by remembering the immensity of God and His passionate love for humanity. Then I ponder the enormity of the universe and countless galaxies. This leads me to my one meager prayer request. My prayer goes something like this. "Father, I know you are incredible, and you made this awesome galaxy of stars and planets. I have just one tiny request. Out of all the millions of galaxies and countless planets, I would like to claim one for Jesus. Out of all the planets of the universe, I would just like to claim the inhabitants of Earth for your Kingdom! I don't want Mars, Jupiter, Venus or beyond; I only want Earth for your glory. I know it's not a big request since there are millions of other planets, many being larger and more impressive. I pray for Your Spirit to release the empowerment within us to take Earth for the Kingdom of God! Amen." What if we had an army of believers all across this planet, filled with Christ's love and compassion for others, pray something similar?

Junkyard Bucket List

Someone asked me recently what my dream car, dream vacation, or an unfulfilled item on my bucket list is. All I could think about is wanting to hear, "Well done." That is all I want for you and for me. Living a life of purpose means fulfilling the call of God on my life. That's it, that's all I want. Truthfully, I know no super mega-vacation will come close to five minutes in Heaven. There is not an exotic sports car or celebrity mansion that remotely compares with the basics Heaven has to offer, so why would I spend my limited efforts on earth chasing such meaningless, trivial trinkets?

The nicest cars of our times will be obsolete and worthless within the foreseeable future. The most extraordinary vacation will be forgotten. People will have devoted their finite energy and time on this earth to something that will be broken down and decaying in a scrap heap or forgotten. All the shiny toys and doodads of this earth that we spend our lives seeking are energy leaks that keep us from attaining true Kingdom riches. Some people spend all their energies on obtaining material things that will ultimately end up in a landfill.

Understand, I'm not against wonderful relaxing vacations, or owning great homes and cars. I'm against those items owning us and consuming our full attention to obtain and maintain them. I love the quote by martyred missionary, Jim Elliot, "He is no fool who gives what he cannot keep to gain that which he cannot lose." [4] Let's make an effort to spend our lives with meaning, seeking Kingdom results of lasting value. I have yet to hear someone at the end of their life saying, "Dang, I wish I wouldn't have spent my whole life serving God. I wish I would have been more materialistic!" However, too many people have voiced regret at the end of their life saying, "I wish I would have done more for the Kingdom." What's on your bucket list?

Ultimate Awards Assembly

Can you envision standing in front of the great white throne of Jesus, where for believers of Jesus the judgment of our works will take place (Revelation 20:11-15)? Can you imagine how you are going to feel when He announces your name? When the names of your family members, teammates, and work associates get called to come before Jesus, our Master, Lord, and Savior? Will you be nervous for your friends and yourself? Expectant?

What will the Master say? Will our life's work get burned up as hay and stubble? (1 Corinthians 3:12-15) Will we be satisfied with our results for the Kingdom, knowing that we did our best to use our talents and abilities to accomplish exactly what God had designed us to do? I like to imagine I'm in the great hall, and since I'm a servant-leader, I feel very concerned about anyone I can influence to hear, "Well done." I'm driven to help my pastor, ministry teammates, business associates, friends, and family all hear, "Well done." I want to be there when you hear, "Well done, thou good and faithful servant!" It is a great honor if, even in only a small way, we can be part of influencing others to achieve the ultimate of all success, hearing, "Well done!"

Empowerment Recap

Our lofty goal throughout this book was to boil down the principle of church, organization, and business growth to one underlying core principle. That is a bold ambition! As we discussed, some churches have individual strengths like an excellent worship service, wonderful outreach ministries, great children's department, missions, or a devoted prayer team, yet they still may not have ongoing Kingdom growth. As you know, I'm for all these things and more, but I believe they should be the outcome of an empowered culture and not the department or ministry in themselves.

The premise that has led us to these conclusions is that we are all God Pods, made in the image of God, and within each one of us are His identity, abilities, and talents that He's given us. When we connect our strengths with the God-given talents of others, we form the Body of Christ. When we allow these characteristics to come together, through the direction of the Holy Spirit to meet people's needs, the abilities of God flow through us to change lives for Kingdom growth. This works because we are carrying out what our Maker intended us to do, so His power and anointing are released through us to accomplish His will. That is why it is imperative that we strategically empower people to release their God-given talents and abilities in a focused direction to meet people's needs. When we do this, we create an empowered culture where great things can happen.

Empowerment Results

This empowered culture will result in individuals fervently seeking to discover, develop, and utilize their skills for Kingdom outcomes. In this environment, people will be praying more than ever, avidly seeking God for revelation knowledge and implementation of His abilities through them. This will ultimately result in every area of our churches and organizations increasing because they would be flooded with the anointing and attributes of God. Imagine every individual attendee and volunteer fully vested in prayer and devotion to fulfill God's call on their life, and ultimately the church or organization they represented. This will result in a congregation of praying, loving, serving people. Our worship services will be a reflection of worshiping before the throne of God. Our children's ministries will be manned by prayed up, devoted men and women. Small groups will be micro-churches, exuding God's love and wisdom. Yes, then we will indeed be the Body of Christ that we were meant to be.

Closing Prayer

I have enjoyed our journey together immensely. I hope that this is not the end, but the launching pad for you.

My prayer would be that we don't just close the book and move back to a hectic meaningless life of completing tasks, seeking to obtain stuff, playing video games, and interacting on social media. I'm praying we will embrace the mission of being empowered to hear, "Well done!" We will achieve this by helping people discover and release the God Pod abilities within them to meet needs that result in Kingdom success. When we become the Empowered Church, we can influence our community, state, nation, and ultimately this planet for Christ!

Chapter 13 Reflection Questions

1. What are your reflections on the story of Jonathan and his armor-bearer? How does it pertain to your relationship with the Holy Spirit?

2. What are three ways that you can facilitate hearing, "Well done," for the people around you?

3. What are your next steps in strategically releasing your follower's God-given talents to meet specific needs?

4. Spend some time visualizing empowerment results in your area of leadership. Write out what you picture happening.